01/20/05

LOUD AND CLEAR

LOUD AND CLEAR

How to Prepare and Deliver Effective Business and Technical Presentations

FOURTH EDITION

George L. Morrisey

Thomas L. Sechrest

Wendy B. Warman

BASIC
BOOKS

A Member of the Perseus Books Group
New York

Many of the designations used by manufacturers and sellers to distinguish their products are claimed as trademarks. Where those designations appear in this book and Perseus Books was aware of a trademark claim, the designations have been printed in initial capital letters (e.g., PowerPoint).

Library of Congress Cataloging-in-Publication Data

Morrisey, George L.
    Loud and clear : how to prepare and deliver effective business and technical presentations / George L. Morrisey, Thomas L. Sechrest, Wendy B. Warman. — 4th ed.
              p.   cm.
    Updated ed. of: Effective business and technical presentations. 3rd ed. 1987
    Includes bibliographical references.
    ISBN 0-201-12793-8
    1. Business presentations. I. Sechrest, Thomas L. II. Warman, Wendy B. III. Morrisey, George L. Effective business and technical presentations. IV. Title.
PN4193.L4M61997
651.7'3—dc21   97-10309
                                                                        CIP

Previous three editions titled *Effective Business and Technical Presentations*

Examples for presentation graphics created by Audio Visual Innovations of Tampa, Florida

Cover design by Suzanne Heiser
Text design by Greg Johnson, Art Directions
Set in 11.5-point Minion by Greg Johnson, Art Directions

15   14   13   12   11   10   9

Contents

Preface ix

CHAPTER 1 Why Read This Book?...1

What's a Presentation? 3

What Are the Most Frequently Made Types
of Presentations?...4

How Is This Book Arranged?...6

Key Points for Making Presentations That Come
Across *Loud and Clear*...8

CHAPTER 2 Preparing Your Presentation 9

Steps in Preparing Your Presentation...10

Practical Application Project...10

STEP 1: Establish Your Objectives 12

How Do Presentation Objectives Differ from
Project Objectives? 12

How Realistic Do Your Presentation Results
Need to Be? 13

What Are Criteria for Determining Your
Presentation Objectives? 15

What Are Secondary Presentation Objectives? 16

Action Exercises 17

STEP 2: Analyze Your Audience 18

What Is the Audience Analysis Audit (AAA)
and How Do You Use It?..19

Action Exercises 22

Audience Analysis Audit (AAA)...................................24

STEP 3: **Prepare a Preliminary Plan**..**27**

    Why Should You Prepare a Preliminary Plan?..........**27**

    How Do You Prepare a Preliminary Plan?.................**28**

    Guidelines for Preparing a Preliminary Plan **30**

    Action Exercises **34**

    Preliminary Plan Worksheet **35**

    Preliminary Plan Examples **38**

STEP 4: **Select Your Resource Material**.............................**42**

    What Should You Include? **42**

    Action Exercises **44**

    Resource Material Worksheet **45**

STEP 5: **Organize Your Material** **47**

    How Does Audience Retention Affect the
        Organization of Your Presentation? **47**

    What Makes a Dynamite OPENING?.........................**49**

    How Can You Cover Your MAIN CONTENT
        without Putting Your Audience to Sleep?...............**53**

    Ten Ways to Make Your Main Content
        More Interesting **53**

    How Can You Make a Powerful CLOSING?..............**56**

    Advantages of Delivering a Convincing Closing......**57**

    Action Exercises **60**

    Guidelines for Organizing Your Material...................**62**

    Presentation Worksheet **64**

    Presentation Outline...**65**

STEP 6: **Practice and Evaluate** **66**

    What Are Some Surefire Methods of
        Practicing?..**67**

    Action Exercises **69**

    Presentation Evaluation Guide..................................**70**

    Summary: Final Thoughts on Preparing Your
        Effective Presentation **74**

CHAPTER 3 Developing and Using Presentation Visuals and Support Materials **77**

  How Will This Chapter Help You? **80**

  STEP 1: Design Your Visuals **81**

      What Is Storyboarding? **85**

      What Should You Illustrate in Your Presentation? **86**

      Who Can Help You? **87**

      What Are Some Effective Approaches for
        Arranging Visuals? **87**

      Where Do You Get Your Visuals? **92**

      Guidelines for Selecting and Designing
        Presentation Visuals **93**

  STEP 2: Display Your Visuals **96**

      Still Images **96**

      How Do You Create Slides and Transparencies? **97**

      Video **98**

      Low-Tech Presentation Support Materials **99**

      Guidelines for Using Presentation Media **103**

  STEP 3: Practice! Practice! Practice! **105**

      Summary: Final Thoughts on Developing
        and Using Presentation Visuals and
        Support Materials **107**

      Action Exercises **108**

      Guidelines for the Effective Use of Visuals and
        Support Materials **110**

      Selected Types of Visuals and Support
        Techniques **112**

CHAPTER 4 Delivering Your Presentation **115**

  What Is the Nature of Communication? **116**

  How Do You Overcome the Fear of Speaking? **117**

  What Presentation Techniques Will Help You
    Present Your Message Better? **120**

What Vocal Techniques Will Enhance Your
Presentation? 125

How Can You Use Common Presentation Tools
Effectively? 129

How and When Do You Handle Audience Questions?...........130

Valuable Tips for Using Presentation Techniques....................141

CHAPTER 5 Handling Presentation Logistics.....................**143**

Has Your Audience Been Satisfactorily Notified?.....................145

How Is the Room Set Up? 145

What About Your Equipment?...148

What About Off-Site Presentations? 149

What Are Some Other Key Issues to Address?...........................150

Presentation Logistics Worksheet...153

CHAPTER 6 In Closing...**157**

Appendix A: Worksheets and Guidelines...............................**163**

Appendix B: Annotated Resources..**185**

About the Authors..**197**

Preface

It has been thirty years since the first edition of this book was published. I am amazed at how its principles for making business and technical presentations continue to guide thousands of individuals and organizations. It is gratifying to think that such continuing demand shows how useful this book's techniques are. There have been many other books written on the subject over the years, most of which focus heavily on presentation skills and the use of visuals. These are important topics of course. My colleagues and I have extensive coverage of both in this book. However, I know of no other book that gives as much attention to *preparation*.

The finest presentation techniques and the most up-to-date visual display will not overcome a poorly prepared message. I believe this approach in *Loud and Clear* has stood the test of time. It emphasizes being certain that you have a clear vision of what you want to *accomplish* with your presentation (not what do you want to say). This approach provides a foundation from which you can design a stronger presentation that is more likely to achieve the results you want with every group you face, whether they are customers, upper management, colleagues, or the general public.

I was fortunate to recruit two presentation experts to co-author this book with me, thus ensuring that it stays as up to date as it is useful. Tom Sechrest (who co-authored the third edition) remains on the leading edge of presentations technology and is able to bring a university perspective to the table. Wendy Warman has been using this approach for several years to train executives and technical professionals to make effective presentations; she knows first hand what corporate America wants and needs in this important arena. This is a book on *planning* and that is my primary area of expertise. As a management consultant and professional speaker for more than 25 years, I have worked with some of the most forward-thinking corporations as well as many of the world's finest speakers and trainers. The synergy in this team has been terrific. The output is much more valuable than what we would have produced individually.

Who Can Benefit from This Book?

While professional speakers will certainly benefit from this book, it has been designed primarily for individuals who are experts in their business or technical fields and who, as part of their responsibilities, must present their ideas to others, inside or outside of their organizations. It is also designed for people who must train or coach these individuals.

Typical of those who would find this a valuable guide are:

▲ *President* of a company or a nonprofit corporation, for a report to the board of directors or stockholders.

▲ *Sales engineer,* for a technical sales presentation to customer representatives.

▲ *Controller,* for an overview of the company's financial projections to a high-level management group.

▲ *Manufacturing cost analyst,* for a review of staff loading requirements with the department manager.

▲ *Research scientist,* for a presentation of the results of a study at a formal gathering of peers (for example, a national symposium) or to management people not specifically oriented to that technical field, two distinctly different types of presentation.

▲ *Government department head,* for presentation of a new initiative to the appropriate legislative body.

▲ *Credit manager,* for introduction of a new credit-application system to employees.

▲ *Training instructor* for presentation of a seminar or workshop.

▲ *Human resource specialist,* for an employee recruitment presentation.

▲ *Project engineer,* for a report on the current status of a directed design change to a customer or to his or her own management.

▲ *Purchasing agent,* for a bid-seeking meeting with potential subcontractors.

▲ *Supervisor,* for a motivational presentation on workmanship to employees.

▲ *Safety engineer,* for an accident-prevention presentation to a group of maintenance supervisors.

▲ *Any technical person,* for a presentation to other technical people or to nontechnical people.

▲ *Any nontechnical person,* for a presentation to technical people or to other nontechnical people.

How Can You, as an Individual, Gain Maximum Benefit from this Book?

Recognizing that many individuals will want or, of necessity, have to use this book without benefit of an accompanying skills-training program, we suggest the following approach for maximum benefit. As with most tools, the versatility and usefulness of this book will increase in direct proportion to your effort and experience in using it. It will be of most value to you if you:

1. Skim through it quickly to get an overview.
2. Then read it carefully, doing the recommended action exercises.
3. Use it as a specific guide every time you make a presentation.
4. Refer to it for solving specific problems only after you are familiar with the total recommended approach.
5. Practice the recommended techniques every chance you get.
6. Start now!

How Can You, as a Presentation Skills Trainer, Use this Book in Your Training Program?

Your personal preferences and experience as an instructor and the particular circumstances of the moment will affect the approach you use in conducting a presentation skills-training program. Our training efforts have been successful when the following points were observed.

1. *Optimum group size:* 12 to 15 persons.

   We have conducted effective classes, however, with as few as seven and as many as 25, in the latter case using a second instructor for divided practice sessions.

2. *Optimum program length:* 21 to 27 hours

   a. Separate sessions of two, three, or four hours (three is the optimum length).

   b. A three-day intensive seminar-workshop.

   c. Combination of half- and full-day sessions.

   The actual program length will be directly related to the number of participants because of the need for individual practice presentations. Also, you could easily expand the program to a full semester in a classroom setting, with greater subject depth and with more and longer practice presentations.

3. *Preparation exercises.*

   a. Preassignment. Participants should come to first session with a presentation topic in mind and with a general knowledge of the subject matter.

   b. Participants should write their presentation objectives in class, followed by small-group evaluation, while you circulate among the groups, assisting as needed.

   c. Each participant should prepare a Preliminary Plan, in or out of class, with in-class, small-group evaluation, while you circulate.

  d. When practical and desirable, participants should design their visuals, in or out of class, for evaluation by other class members as well as by you as the instructor.

4. *Practice presentations by participants.*

  a. Each participant should make at least two in-class presentations of 10- to 15-minute duration. Some variation, either shorter or longer, is possible without loss of value. Our experience indicates that individual learning is much greater with two or more practice presentations than with a single practice presentation, because of the opportunity to correct presentation errors.

  b. We strongly recommend videotaping the practice presentations, with the opportunity for later review and evaluation with you as the instructor/coach or for self-evaluation by the presenter individually.

  c. Audiotape recording is an acceptable alternative if video is not available, recognizing that evaluation is limited to the voice and verbal message only.

  d. We recommend that you prepare both a written and a verbal evaluation, as the instructor, and by fellow participants, immediately following each practice presentation to provide instant feedback to the presenter as well as cumulative learning for all participants. (One technique that we have found effective is to rotate a "chief evaluator" role among participants, giving each the opportunity to evaluate constructively someone else's presentation. You can supplement this with your own comments as well as comments from other participants.)

5. Instructional approach.

  a. You need to be a role model, demonstrating a variety of visuals and other aids and presentation approaches during your formal subject matter presentations.

  b. Cover each of the six presentation steps completely detailed in Chapter 2, with supervised action exercises, before you proceed with practice presentations.

    c. Encourage participants to read Chapter 3, **Developing and Using Presentation Visuals and Support Materials**, on their own, with an option of a separate, supervised workshop session on preparing visuals.

    d. Schedule practice presentations to start as quickly as possible after you cover preparation steps and related exercises, making initial assignments during the first session.

    e. Develop a series of short discussions on presentation techniques that can be interspersed as a change of pace between groups of practice presentations.

    f. When feasible, schedule one-on-one coaching reviews with participants using the video- or audiotapes recorded during practice sessions.

Please bear in mind that these factors have proved effective in training programs that we have conducted. You may be equally successful using a different combination. You can adapt the material in this book easily to almost any approach.

Acknowledgments

Our appreciation, as always, goes first to the many participants in our seminars on this and related topics who have "forced" us to continue improving the approach. In addition, we have received constructive feedback from many individuals and organizations that have used earlier editions of this book, identifying "soft" and confusing areas that needed expansion or fine-tuning.

Our special thanks go to Jeanine Fischer, Stephenie Scanlon, and Martin Schaffel of AVI (Audio Visual Innovations) in Tampa, Florida, for their creative assistance with the visuals included in this book.

We also appreciate the feedback we received from several people during the manuscript phase for this edition, which resulted in several modifications we believe significantly added to its value. These include Harold Burke and Matt Vance as well as professional colleagues Dianna Booher, Bert Decker, Rick Gilbert, Kathleen Hessert, and Ed Scannell.

George L. Morrisey
Merritt Island, Florida
March 1997

CHAPTER

1

Why Read This Book?

Presentations. Briefings. Sales demonstrations. Training programs. Slide shows. White papers. How many of the following thoughts went through your mind while you sat through sessions like these?

▲ This is *sooooo* boring!

▲ What is she talking about?

▲ Where's he going with this?

▲ Why are we all here?

▲ Poor guy! He's hating this almost as much as I am.

▲ I've got better things to do with my time than listen to this!

Let's flip the coin now. What were your feelings the last time *you* were asked to make a presentation?

▲ *Panic!* What should I say?

▲ How can I ever pull it all together?

▲ How can I connect with this audience?

▲ How can I make sure I achieve the results I want?

When you prepare your next presentation, this book will help you systematically answer these questions and make sure that members of your audience don't ask themselves questions like those in the first set.

Why do many managers and technical experts, extremely competent in their own fields, nevertheless make these mistakes when they try to convey their ideas to others?

▲ They forget to use an analytical approach in their presentations, even though that is an integral part of their everyday work.

▲ They do a *data dump* instead of making a clearly designed and focused presentation.

▲ They revert to their own jargon, regardless of the audience's level of understanding.

▲ They think too little about the needs of their audience.

Regardless of your current experience level in making presentations, you can increase your effectiveness significantly by following the simple analytical approach described in this book. While it may be simple, it does not mean this approach will be easy. It will require discipline that may seem somewhat foreign to you. However, the potential payoff can be enormous.

Here are **seven tangible benefits** you'll receive when you use this analytical approach, benefits that will go a long way toward making your presentation come across *loud and clear*. You can expect to:

1. Reduce your stress and anxiety about making a presentation.

2. Cut your average presentation length in half.

3. Reduce your preparation time by 20 to 50 percent.

4. Reduce or at least contain the number and complexity of charts and visuals you use so that *you*, not your charts, are seen as the primary source of information.

5. Increase your audience's interest, understanding, and involvement.

6. Connect more directly with your audience's needs and wants.

7. Significantly improve your results in a way that will pay off handsomely for both your organization and you personally.

What's a Presentation?

Everyone has a general idea of what's meant by a *presentation*. But let's define the term more specifically. A presentation involves the preparation and delivery of essential subject matter in a logical, condensed form, leading to *productive results*. The components that contribute significantly to the effectiveness of a presentation are shown in the accompanying diagram.

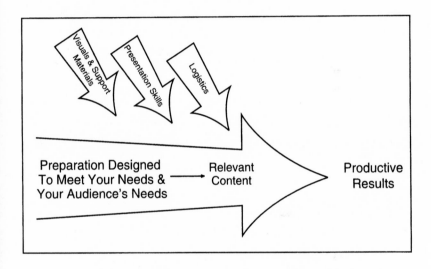

- ▲ **Preparation** involves the selection and development of technical information designed to meet both your needs and your audience's needs. Recognize that your needs and your audience's needs are likely to be quite different. The only way *your* needs will be met is if your audience feels *their* needs are being met.

- ▲ **Relevant content** is at the heart of your presentation. Why? Because technical information that is not focused on meeting the needs of your audience frequently becomes a *data dump* that does little more than demonstrate your knowledge of the subject.

- ▲ **Visuals and support materials, presentation skills,** and **logistics** *support* the relevant content. Understanding the *support role* of these elements is essential. If you compromise content in order to exploit unusual visuals or gimmicks, to deliver the material in a particular way (such as with a spontaneous live demonstration), or to use a less than optimal meeting site, you might enhance your audience's acceptance of your presentation temporarily. In the long run, however, you run the risk of not communicating your message effectively and therefore not accomplishing your presentation's real objectives.

▲ **Productive results** is the goal of any presentation. Simply defined, this means getting your message across *loud and clear* in a manner that will accomplish your objectives with this specific audience.

And how do you know when you have made an effective presentation? If your audience does what you want them to do as a result of your presentation, you have accomplished your objectives, even if you violated many of the principles covered in this book.

What Are the Most Frequently Made Types of Presentations?

There are four distinctive, though at times overlapping, types of presentations you may be called on to give.

1. **Persuasive.** Every presentation is, to a certain extent, persuasive. First and foremost, you must convince your audience that you know what you're talking about. Beyond this, you might use a persuasive presentation to:
   - **Pique the interest** of a potential customer (or group of customers) in a new product, service, capability, or program that you are offering or will offer.
   - **Gain an audience's confidence** in the organization you represent and the message you are presenting.

- **Convince upper management** of the need to commit additional personnel or money or to use a particular methodology.
- **Sell an existing customer** on a new product, the modification of a current product or service, or a change in scope, funding, scheduling, or procedures.
- **Persuade colleagues,** employees, or members of parallel organizations to accept changes or to acknowledge the need for closer coordination.

2. **Explanatory.** An explanatory presentation provides a general familiarization, gives "the big picture," or describes new developments. Your primary objective is to make new information available or to refresh your audience's understanding of a given topic. This type of presentation rarely involves a high level of detail. It might be used to:

- **Orient new employees** to your organization.
- **Acquaint staff members** with what's involved in opening a new branch or division.
- **Provide general information** relevant to the needs of another department, company, or agency.
- **Present information** to a professional association, civic organization, or other group in the interest of good public relations.

3. **Instructional.** This type of presentation teaches others how to use something, such as a new procedure or piece of equipment. This usually requires greater involvement of your audience to reinforce their learning and frequently provides detailed information. Typical uses for an instructional presentation are to:

- **Instruct customers** in the use of specific processes or equipment.
- **Train customer representatives** to instruct their own employees in the use of specific processes or equipment.

- **Teach others** within your organization to follow specific procedures.
- **Coach employees** in the use of specific software.

4. **Briefing.** A briefing usually brings your audience up to date on something with which they are already familiar. Details may be provided on a selective basis, according to the needs and interests of a specific audience. A briefing may be designed to:

- **Update customer representatives** on the status of a specific project.
- **Inform management** on current expenditures compared to budget.
- **Provide a detailed accounting** of the progress of a work group chartered to conduct an investigation or a research project.
- **Clarify modifications** to a particular product or service.

How Is This Book Arranged?

The diagram shown earlier in the chapter represents the major inputs that directly affect the quality of your presentation: selective use of information designed to meet both your needs and your audience's needs, which leads to relevant content; supported by visuals and techniques; with careful attention to logistical details; culminating in productive results. The diagram also reflects the organization of this book.

Developing relevant content is dealt with in Chapter 2, which describes a six-step presentation-design model, each step of which is critical for planning the content of your presentations. These six steps are:

1. **Establish your objectives.**

2. **Analyze your audience.**

3. **Prepare a preliminary plan.**

4. Select your resource material.

5. Organize your material.

6. **Practice and evaluate** your presentation in advance and make any necessary modifications.

Overlooking any one of these six steps may lead to serious flaws or gaps in the final presentation. Recognizing that content is the foundation on which the effectiveness of your presentation is based, Chapter 2, on preparation, is the longest in the book and deserves the greatest attention.

The benefits and limitations of common visuals and other support materials, and how you can use them to improve the effectiveness of your presentation, are dealt with in Chapter 3. The visual sophistication of audiences and the increasing availability of new and often complex presentation tools requires that this subject be given special attention. Even though visuals clearly play a secondary role (that of *supporting* your presentation's content), the use of poorly designed visuals or failure to employ them skillfully can destroy an otherwise good presentation.

Both Chapters 2 and 3 contain action exercises to enhance your understanding and use of this approach. These exercises enable you to select a presentation topic that is relevant to your own needs and to work actively on designing your presentation's content and developing its visuals and other supporting materials.

Presentation techniques, the prime factors to consider in delivering your message, are covered in Chapter 4, which focuses on overcoming fear of speaking, improving your presentation skills (what to do with your hands, for example), and vocal techniques, as well as your interaction with your audience, including how to handle various types of audience questions.

The often-overlooked logistical details associated with your presentation are the topic of Chapter 5, which outlines arrangements for everything from delivering a simple boardroom report to staging a major off-site event.

Appendix B, "Annotated Resources," contains other resources that may be useful at various stages of your preparation and delivery process.

Key Points for Making Presentations That Come Across *Loud and Clear*

You can substantially improve the effectiveness of your presentations by following the logical and proven approach covered in this book. This includes:

▲ Understanding and using the six-step approach for effective preparation.

▲ Selecting and developing relevant content, designed to meet your needs and your audience's needs, that leads to productive results.

▲ Making effective use of visuals and other support materials.

▲ Becoming more skillful in the use of proven presentation techniques.

▲ Paying attention to the logistics of your presentation.

If you follow this approach, it will result in more concise and productive presentations that come across *loud and clear.* The payoff on your investment will be tremendous.

CHAPTER
2
Preparing Your Presentation

Managing your presentation is no different from managing any other kind of investment. In allocating certain resources—primarily ideas, time, and personal energy, in this case—you expect to get a return that will exceed the value of your investment. In other words, you anticipate that your presentation, if successful, will result in something of value for you and for your audience. Defining your anticipated result and designing your presentation to accomplish that result is the focus of this chapter.

Careful thought during your planning stages may cause you to realize that your goals might be accomplished more efficiently and productively by some means *other* than a presentation. Often a letter, a telephone call, or a technical bulletin will achieve the productive results you are looking for.

In considering a presentation as your communication approach rather than one of these other alternatives, you introduce critical cost factors, which involve both the cost of your presentation itself and the value of the *time* of everyone involved—you as the presenter, people providing support, and your audience as well. These significant cost factors must weigh heavily in your choice of how to achieve your communication goal.

When your analysis indicates that a formal presentation is justified, we strongly recommend a six-step planning process that breaks down the preparation into manageable units. These six steps are designed to help you produce a shorter, clearer, and more productive presentation in less time. Each of these steps plays a vital role in the process, and you should not overlook any step.

Steps in Preparing Your Presentation

1. Establish your objectives.
2. Analyze your audience.
3. Prepare a preliminary plan.
4. Select your resource material.
5. Organize your material.
6. Practice and evaluate.

You may already follow a number of these steps intuitively in preparing your presentations. This chapter clearly defines the steps and the interrelationship among them and illustrates their practical application. This way, you can follow the process as an *integrated system,* thereby providing you with the maximum benefit.

Following the identification of your practical application project in the next section, we'll examine these six steps, one at a time, in the balance of the chapter, devoting a separate section to each.

Practical Application Project

Since people must be actively involved to learn best, we have provided action exercises for each of the six steps in this chapter. (Another group of action exercises on the use of visuals and support materials appears at the end of Chapter 3.) At this point, we recommend that you select a topic that you might be required to make a presentation on in the near future and then, using this topic throughout, complete the action exercises. If it's easier for you to think in terms of a specific simulated situation, here are some possibilities.

▲ You must **deliver a sales presentation** to a prospective internal or external customer.

▲ Your supervisor and your peers need **a report on the current status** of your major assignment.

▲ You want to **recruit a group of talented prospects** by outlining the merits of joining your organization.

▲ You have been asked to **make a presentation to a civic group** on the mission and function of your organization.

▲ You must **make a case to upper management** for a budget increase for your project.

The more practical you can make your selected topic, the more valuable the action exercises will be. Once you have chosen your topic, follow the six steps in order to insure that your presentation comes across *loud and clear.*

▶STEP 1: Establish Your Objectives

Without a doubt, establishing objectives is the most important step in the planning process. Surprisingly, it is the one most often overlooked. Step 1 is designed to answer the question, "Why am I making this presentation?"—not "What am I going to say?" Start by determining what it is you want to *accomplish* with your presentation. In other words, "What reaction do I want from this audience?" or "What do I want this audience to do as a result of this presentation?" These are short-term, self-centered objectives that you may or may not choose to share with your audience. For example, if your objective is to leave the meeting with a signed contract, you may not wish to state that expectation until after you have completed all or most of your presentation.

How Do Presentation Objectives Differ from Project Objectives?

There is a natural tendency to confuse the objectives of what you are proposing in the presentation with the objectives of your presentation itself. **THEY ARE NOT THE SAME!** One is the **project objective**; the other is the **presentation objective**. To understand the **project objective**, ask yourself, "What will happen if the proposal or project is successful?" To understand the **presentation objective**, ask yourself, "What will happen if my presentation is successful?" For example, in a new-product proposal to top management, a project objective might be "to obtain additional profitable business for the company." However, the presentation objective might be "to get approval to proceed with the project." A project objective for a new job-training program in the Department of Labor might be "to provide unemployed citizens with the skills necessary to get and keep a job." A presentation objective on the program might be "to initiate action on a demographic study of potential participants" or "to get a budgetary allocation for Phase 1."

Clearly understanding the difference between project and presentation objectives is absolutely vital. The first stated objective in each of the two examples is an admirable long-range achievement and would undoubtedly be a significant part of your presentation. However, your presentation cannot, by itself, accomplish the long-range goal. It can only initiate action toward that goal. Therefore, you must identify what your presentation can accomplish, if successful, and focus your efforts toward that end. If you do not accomplish the short-term objectives for your presentation, you're not likely to achieve the long-range objectives of your project, either.

Presentation Objectives

▲ Why are you making this presentation?

▲ What reaction do you want from this audience?

▲ What do you want this audience to do afterward?

NOT What are you going to say?

Your presentation objectives give firm direction to your preparation process. Instead of following the normal initial impulse to wade through reports, studies, charts, and so forth, much of which will be tossed aside later—you can make better use of your time at the beginning by focusing on selecting information that will lead to the specific outcome you want.

How Realistic Do Your Presentation Results Need to Be?

It's important to keep in mind the *specific* results you expect from your presentation. To the extent that you can control how, when, and to whom you will make your presentation, the results you identify should be:

▲ **Realistic in scope,** so you can accomplish them in both the preparation time and the presentation time you have available. You are far better off effectively presenting one major step of a program, opening the door for later presentations, than trying to cover the waterfront, so to speak, and run the risk of overwhelming your audience. Making your presentation in well-prepared, comprehensible segments is often the key to their acceptance of your ideas.

▲ **Realistic in view of your audience's knowledge and experience.** Does your audience have the knowledge and experience that will enable them to achieve the results you want? Presenting the applications of a new system in technical terms would probably be inadvisable for a group of executives (unless they are all as technically literate as you are). A preliminary presentation on terminology might be in order or perhaps a broad, results-oriented presentation, with the provision to cover certain technical aspects later, after audience members feel knowledgeable about the subject.

Objectives Need to Be

▲ Realistic in scope.
▲ Realistic for what your audience now knows.
▲ Realistic for what your audience can do.
▲ Realistic in terms of what you can accomplish.

▲ **Realistic in view of your audience's ability to act.** Do the members of your audience have the authority to make the decisions you would like? For example, if you are making a presentation on a new inventory control system to a group of first-line supervisors, it would be unrealistic to propose the purchase of a particular type of software to this audience. They are not likely to be able to make such a decision. However, making a presentation that encourages them to acquire a greater familiarity with the process and its benefits would certainly be realistic.

▲ **Realistic in terms of what you can reasonably expect to accomplish.** A costly plan of action may prove to be the ideal solution in a given situation. However, you might find that such factors as budget, personnel, floor space, or insurmountable resistance by key individuals will make acceptance of your proposal unlikely. It might be better to set as your immediate objective the approval of a "stripped-down" version of the plan that could lay the groundwork for gaining approval of the more costly solution at a later date.

What Are Criteria for Determining Your Presentation Objectives?

Your presentation objectives should be specific and meet *one or more* of the following criteria:

1. They should answer the question, "Why am I making this presentation?"
   Example: *This is a regular monthly update to upper management on the status of the XYZ project. I want to show them how to spot potential problems so that they can take corrective action.*

2. They should state the results desired from the presentation—in effect, completing the sentence, "I want the following things to happen as a result of this presentation . . ."
   Example: *The customer will recognize the benefits of our new product and agree to make a purchase.*

3. If it's important to identify the specific project to be presented, your objective should be specific in terms of the results expected. "I want to tell about . . . so that . . . will take place."
   Example: *I want to explain the new inventory control system so that my team members will recognize its value to them in terms of increased efficiency and will realize that it will not be a threat to their jobs.*

Keeping in mind the requirements for clear presentation objectives, review the sample objectives in this subsection as models for your own presentation.

If your principal topic is the "need for a new inventory control system" your presentation objectives might be:

1. *To create an awareness of the need for the new system.*

2. *To gain management approval and support for the new system so that:*

   a. *They will authorize the necessary funds.*

   b. *They will approve the allocation of sufficient time for people to learn and implement the system.*

   c. *They will approve implementation of the new system both verbally and in writing.*

If you plan to make a presentation on the "support role of the financial department," your objective might be:

1. *To explain the support functions of the financial department to line managers so they will:*

   a. *Recognize and use those services available to them.*

   b. *Accept guidance from financial department staff as desirable and helpful.*

   c. *Seek assistance before rather than after problems occur.*

   d. *Provide positive feedback that will enable the financial department to improve its services.*

What Are Secondary Presentation Objectives?

In addition to your presentation's primary objectives, you may expect certain secondary results from your presentation that you may or may not wish to share with your audience. Identifying them will remind you of their importance even if they are not communicated. Here are some examples of secondary presentation objectives:

▲ *To establish my personal credibility in this presentation, regardless of the outcome, so that my future presentations will be favorably received.*

▲ *To make my audience aware of and responsive to the other products, services, and capabilities offered by my department or organization.*

▲ *To share information with employees that may relieve anxieties over possible production cutbacks.*

▲ *To create ongoing awareness of the need for increased support for project ABC.*

Failure to disclose your secondary objectives openly is not meant to be devious. Rather, you need to determine if your objectives might be jeopardized by revealing them.

When clear, specific, and realistic presentation as well as project objectives are established, your "preparation energy" will be focused on achieving *results*. In other words, you will increase the probability that your message will come through *loud and clear*.

Action Exercises

1. Using the topic you selected earlier in the chapter, write a short, clear statement of your objectives compatible with the criteria outlined.

2. When you are reasonably satisfied with your objectives statement, ask some of your co-workers to read it and provide feedback. Do not give them any other comment or explanation. If, after reading the objectives once, they understand exactly what you are trying to accomplish with the presentation, you have successfully completed what is probably the most important—and perhaps the most difficult—step in the preparation process. If they raise objections that seem valid to you, rewrite your objectives to reflect their suggestions, using your own good judgment.

▶ STEP 2: Analyze Your Audience

The first step, establishing your presentation objectives, focused on satisfying your own needs—determining what you, as the presenter, want to accomplish. This second step, audience analysis, reverses that point of view, focusing on your audience's needs and wants. What do you need to know about your audience's knowledge, attitudes, likes, and dislikes in order to increase the probability of achieving your objectives? What is likely to move your audience to do what you want them to do?

Many well-prepared presentations have fallen short of their objectives because the presenter failed to anticipate how the audience would react. For instance, one organization prepared what were basically good presentations for a group of top-level government officials. For the first four months, though, the reception from this group of officials was rather cool. The presenters were perplexed. The material was what the officials had requested. And the presenters had prepared what they thought were excellent visuals, using cartoon figures to build interest—a technique that can be very effective. In this case, however, the key official simply disliked cartoons. This personal idiosyncrasy and the chilling effect it had on the rest of the audience kept the presenters from achieving their presentation objectives. A short preliminary outline of the presentation or a brief discussion of the format with one or two of the officials during the planning stage might have prevented this problem. In any case, after the first presentation proved less than successful, the presenters should have made a real attempt to determine why.

Although you use this second step primarily before you make your presentation, you must also must realize that you may have to do some audience analysis on the spot and make modifications to your presentation based on data that were not available to you earlier. The more thorough your advance planning, though, the fewer on-the-spot adjustments you should have to make.

There are also many audiences for whom the type of detailed analysis described here would not be necessary. Regardless of the amount of detail required, you must carefully consider your audience's viewpoint as you plan your presentation.

What Is the Audience Analysis Audit (AAA) and How Do You Use It?

The best way to picture your audience and to target your presentation specifically to them is to complete the **Audience Analysis Audit (AAA)** (shown on page 24). When you complete this worksheet for a specific presentation you are planning, it will help you identify your audience's characteristics and keep them in mind throughout your planning process. This will increase the likelihood that your content will appropriately involve and inform your audience, leading to a greater probability that you will achieve your presentation objectives. Another advantage in using this worksheet is that it helps you develop an opening that addresses your audience so that you get their attention and dispel any reservations they may have about the information you are about to present.

The AAA is divided into six beneficial parts, each of which provides information for a specific use:

1. **Identify your objectives for this audience**, which you did in Step 1. Knowing what you want to accomplish as a result of this presentation will highlight many of the specific audience characteristics you need to be aware of. Always keep your objectives in mind as you move through your planning process. Remember that a presentation on the same topic for two different audiences may require different objectives for each group.

2. **Identify your audience's expected benefits and positive outcomes**, to satisfy your audience's WIIFM ("What's in it for me?"). When your audience understands the benefit of listening to your presentation, there's a greater chance they will pay closer attention to what you're saying.

3. **Identify the desired emotional effects on your audience.**
Ask yourself, "How do I want my audience to *feel* as a
result of my presentation?" For example, if you want them
to feel excited about the potential of the new system and
about how it will improve their business, this goal will
influence your selection of examples and illustrations
designed to create such excitement. It's also important to
express this excitement in your opening statement to
ensure that you will achieve your desired effects.

4. **Analyze this specific audience,** to provide insight into the
kind of *overall approach* most likely to achieve your objectives with this particular audience and to clarify the *scope*
of the material you will select. Your analysis should help
you determine how deep into your subject you need to go
from the point of view of this specific audience.

5. **Identify appropriate information and techniques.** What
kinds of information, techniques, or approaches are most
likely to have a positive effect on this particular audience?
What kinds might result in negative reactions? (Better
analysis in the area of techniques might have prevented the
cartoon fiasco referred to on page 18.)

6. **Summarize the most important information.** In addition
to a general summary of the information, you may wish to
highlight areas in this section that could be sensitive when
you are presenting. For example, if you determine from
your audience analysis that your audience's opinion about
you, your organization, or the subject is slightly or openly
hostile, that should alert you to address the reason for this
hostility right up front. Doing this will provide you with a
connection to your audience, not a disconnection right
from the start. You might begin with an opening statement
such as this, "I'm aware, after talking with several of you,
that you have some significant concerns about the new system. I assure you that, after my presentation, you'll feel
more comfortable with it and you'll see how beneficial it
will be to you and your work team." Right up front you've

Ways to Assess Your Audience

▲ Talk to others who have presented to them.

▲ Talk with members of the audience.

▲ Review the audience's recent work.

▲ Review your past presentation.

▲ Listen to your common sense.

---

brought their concerns and resistance out in the open. Your audience will be more receptive to your presentation when you address these issues in your opening statements.

At this stage in the presentation process, you should be alert for any additional relevant characteristics of your particular audience, not identified in the AAA, that you may also wish to investigate.

Here are five helpful ways you can gather information that will help you complete your Audience Analysis Audit (AAA):

▲ You can consult with other individuals or groups who have made presentations to the same audience.

▲ You can either speak directly with selected audience members or form your impressions indirectly by consulting with their colleagues.

▲ You can review examples of the work of your audience members.

▲ You can debrief after each presentation and assess that audience's reactions.

▲ You can apply common sense to what you already know about the situation and this particular audience.

If you're not able to contact your audience members ahead of time or consult with someone who knows them, you may wish to survey your audience at the beginning of your presentation *before your opening statements*. This will allow you to adjust your content and delivery. Ask audience members some direct, well-rehearsed questions. For example, you may want to know how much information your listeners might already have on the new system you'll

Questions About Your Audience

▲ What are your objectives for them?

▲ How should they feel after your presentation?

▲ What will turn them on or off?

▲ What is the best way to reach them?

be speaking about. Simply ask, "Let me see by a show of hands how many have received some general information on the new system?" You may also want to ask something like, "How many are actually using the system?" This will let you know how much detail to go into. It may also tell you who may have already formed opinions, and, consequently, you may want to find out their likes or dislikes about the system.

Audiences will respect you and will be impressed by your effort to make your presentation relevant to them. It's also a great way to build rapport with an audience that doesn't know you. These questions will help you confirm that you won't present information that your audience already knows or has no interest in knowing. In other words, your presentation will be right on target to correspond with the needs and wants of this specific audience.

Take a systematic approach to analyze your audience so that you not only avoid as many problems as possible, but also plan a presentation that is most likely to accomplish your objectives with *this* audience. If you get into trouble with your presentation, it might be because you failed to pay enough attention to your AAA.

Action Exercises

1. Using the Audience Analysis Audit (AAA) as a guide, and supplying whatever additional information about the audience you feel would be helpful, write a brief profile or general description of the audience for whom you are

preparing the presentation, using the topic you selected earlier.

2. Review your analysis or observations with a few of your co-workers to determine whether they would agree that your profile is as accurate as possible.

3. Identify in writing the specific audience for whom you are designing your presentation and give a short, one- or two-sentence summary of *pertinent* information about their knowledge, attitudes, and so forth.

Audience Analysis Audit (AAA)

(Fill in the blanks or circle the most descriptive terms.)

1. Identify your objectives for this audience. What do you want the members of your audience to do as a result of this presentation?

_____

_____

2. Identify your audience's expected benefits and positive outcomes. What will they want to have happen as a result of your presentation?

_____

_____

3. Identify the desired emotional effects on your audience. How do you want your audience to feel as a result of your presentation?

_____

_____

4. Analyze this specific audience. What do you need to know about them?

- What is their occupational relationship to you or to the organization you represent?

  Customers   Top management   Public

  Co-workers   Employees   Suppliers

  Other (describe): _____

- How long have they been in this relationship with you or the organization you represent?

  _____

- What is their level of understanding of the types of information you will be sharing?

  Technical   Nontechnical   Generally high

  Generally low   Unknown

- How willing are the members of this audience to accept the ideas you will present?

  Eager   Receptive   Neutral

  Slightly resistant   Strongly resistant   Unknown

- What is their knowledge of the subject?

  High   Moderate   Limited

  None   Unknown

- What are their opinions about you or the organization you represent?

  Very favorable   Positive   Neutral

  Slightly hostile   Openly hostile   Unknown

- What are their opinions about the subject?

  Very favorable   Positive   Neutral

  Slightly hostile   Openly hostile   Unknown

- What are their roles related to what you are presenting?

  Decision-makers   Decision-influencers Doers

  Unknown   Other:_____

- Why are they attending this presentation?

  _____

  _____

- List some of the advantages and disadvantages of the presentation objectives to the members of this audience as individuals.

  Advantages: _____

  _____

  _____

  Disadvantages: _____

  _____

  _____

5. Identify appropriate information and techniques.

- What types of information or techniques are most likely to capture the attention of this audience?

  High-tech   Statistical comparisons   Cost-related

  Anecdotes   Demonstrations

  Others (describe): _____

- What information or techniques are most likely to get negative reactions from this audience? _____

  _____

6. Summarize the most important information from the preceding five sections.

_____

_____

_____

_____

_____

_____

_____

_____

_____

_____

_____

_____

_____

_____

_____

_____

_____

_____

_____

▶ STEP 3: Prepare a Preliminary Plan

This may be the single most valuable step in this process. You need to complete this *before* you decide exactly how to put your presentation together. *The Preliminary Plan is not designed to be a speaking outline;* rather, it is a conceptual guide to help you determine what actions will most logically lead to accomplishing your presentation objectives. Think of it as a blueprint for your presentation. Its purpose is to build a framework on which you can develop your ideas and decide how much and what kind of information you will need.

Why Should You Prepare a Preliminary Plan?

▲ The plan forces you, the presenter, to carefully assess the direction to take, from selection of your subject matter to keeping the flow of your ideas focused, and where to emphasize for the best results.

▲ The plan establishes the framework within which support personnel who provide backup data, prepare visuals, or assist in the presentation itself must work. Many of us have had the experience of assigning such responsibility to someone and having the work done all wrong, in terms of what we had in mind. The Preliminary Plan, if it is properly prepared, minimizes this problem, because it gives both you and your support personnel specific *written* guidelines for completing the preparation process.

One caution: Only a rare individual can deliver an effective presentation that has been entirely prepared by someone else. If you will be delivering the presentation, you must be actively involved at least in preparing the Preliminary Plan, so that you can provide direction for the concepts and approaches to be used. Only in this way will the final message reflect your own convictions, personality, and ability. Many well-planned presentations have failed to produce their desired results because they were given by someone who did not have a part in their preparation. If you lack sufficient time or motivation to contribute meaningfully to the preparation of the Preliminary Plan, perhaps it would be better for someone else to make the presentation.

How Do You Prepare a Preliminary Plan?

The guidelines shown on pages 30–31 and the worksheet included at the end of this section are perhaps the *most* useful tools in this entire text. Presenters who have based successful presentations on these guidelines often keep a copy in some prominent spot where they can readily refer to them when they need to prepare or modify a presentation.

Effectively using these guidelines on an ongoing basis will also enhance your ability to prepare a presentation on extremely short notice, even as little as 20 minutes—an important benefit!

The first and second guidelines, related to your objectives and audience analysis (Steps 1 and 2 of this preparation process), are the foundation for the remaining guidelines. Guideline 3 is really the heart of your Preliminary Plan. It calls for stating your *main ideas or concepts* that your audience *must comprehend* if you are to accomplish your presentation objectives.

You should write your main ideas as statements in conclusion form. These conclusions should be the ones you want your audience to reach based on what you are presenting. These statements should *not* merely identify subjects to be covered, such as cost, schedule, or organizational capabilities; *they should spell out what you want your audience to BELIEVE about these topics.* These may or may not be statements of fact. But they should provide guidance for the kinds of facts you want to present. Here are some examples related to the subjects of cost, schedule, and organizational capabilities.

▲ *The cost is reasonable and will have a significant payoff in the future.*

▲ *We can meet our deadlines.*

▲ *Engineering is capable of performing the necessary design work.*

Frequently, there may be just one main idea in your presentation, even though you may approach it from several angles. You may wish to stress only the idea that "we will meet our primary objectives in spite of certain temporary setbacks," but you may want to do so in a number of different ways to make your point.

Normally, you will present no more than five main ideas if you want your audience to remember them. If it's necessary to communicate more ideas in order to achieve some specific objectives, it might be preferable to present them at two separate meetings: the first, an overview or a request for input, and the second, a bid for a favorable decision.

The fourth guideline requires you to identify the types of factual information you need to support and clarify your main ideas. This is the information that will get and keep your audience's attention because it relates directly to them. Keep details to a minimum, unless your presentation is instructional or is meant to provide specific information in an area where your audience is already familiar.

Guidelines for Preparing a Preliminary Plan

Use the Preliminary Plan as a guide:

▲ For you, as the presenter, in selecting your materials, keeping your ideas focused, and determining key emphasis points.

▲ For support personnel who may provide you with backup data, prepare visuals, or assist in the presentation itself.

1. **Identify your specific objectives for this presentation,** keeping in mind one or more of the following criteria:

   • They should answer the question, "Why am I making this presentation?"

   • They should state the results you want from the presentation—in effect, completing the sentence, "I want the following things to happen as a result of this presentation: . . ."

   • If you need to identify the specific project in your objectives, use a sentence such as, "I want to tell about . . . so that . . . will take place."

   • Your objectives should take into consideration any secondary objectives that you want to accomplish with your presentation.

2. **Identify the specific audience** for whom you are designing this presentation. State in one or two sentences the pertinent information about the audience's expectations, knowledge, attitudes, and so forth.

3. **State the main ideas or concepts** that your audience *must* comprehend if you are to meet your presentation objectives. These should:

   • Be in conclusion form and, preferably, in complete sentences.

   • Definitely lead to the accomplishment of your specific objectives.

- Be interesting in themselves or capable of being made so.
- Be few in number, usually no more than five.

4. **Identify necessary factual information** to support each of your main ideas and make them comprehensible to your audience. Avoid excessive detail.

The following example explains a proposed reorganization to managers. It is a two-session presentation, because there is more to be covered than a single meeting can effectively address. We have identified the main ideas for the first session, followed by the types of factual information required to support each main idea. We have repeated this for the second session as well.

First Session: Main Ideas

1. Changes taking place in our primary market will significantly affect our profitability.
2. We are evaluating our organizational structure in order to reduce overhead costs.
3. There will be no reduction in personnel as a result of any reorganization.
4. Based on the guidelines provided, each department head will make recommendations about how best to reduce or contain costs.

First Session: Supporting Information

Main Idea 1—(Changes taking place in our primary market...)

▲ Sales figures for several previous years, showing decreasing profits.

▲ Information about competitors' products, including retail costs and sales volumes.

▲ Market projections by analysts, detailing expected trends.

Main Idea 2—(We are evaluating our organizational structure ...)

▲ Overhead costs for several previous years, showing continual increases.

▲ Estimated costs for future years if the present administrative structure is maintained.

▲ Detailed cost figures for the units in which the largest overhead increases have taken place.

Main Idea 3—(There will be no reduction in personnel ...)

▲ Units where employees will be affected and how these employees could be reassigned.

▲ Plans for retaining affected employees.

Main Idea 4—(... each department head will make recommendations ...)

▲ Areas in which cost might be reduced or contained.

▲ Types of recommendations expected from each department.

Second Session: Main Ideas

1. We will contract with a management consulting firm for an analysis of cost-reduction or cost-containment alternatives.

2. Company A has been awarded the contract based on its experience with this type of assignment.

3. XYZ unit will coordinate the efforts of the consulting firm.

4. Each department head will be responsible for evaluating the completed analysis.

5. Final recommendations will be made at the end of six months.

Second Session: Supporting Information

Main Idea 1—(We will contract with ...)

▲ Reasons for the decision.

Main Idea 2—(Company A has been awarded the contract ...)

▲ Reasons for the selection.

▲ Background information on Company A.

Main Idea 3—(XYZ unit will coordinate ...)

▲ Rationale behind the choice of the XYZ unit as coordinator.

▲ Procedures for the work to be conducted by the consulting firm.

Main Idea 4—(Each department head will be responsible ...)

▲ Suggested evaluation procedures.

▲ Key indicators to look for.

Main Idea 5—(Final recommendations will be made ...)

▲ How recommendations will be evaluated.

▲ Implementation timetable.

As you can see, the main ideas, as stated in the Preliminary Plan, may or may not be facts in themselves. They don't have to be. They must, however, be conclusions that can be reached on the basis of the factual information presented.

You can easily see from this example how necessary the Preliminary Plan is in making sure your presentation comes across *loud and clear* and in successfully accomplishing your presentation objectives. To consolidate the elements of your Preliminary Plan, you may wish to use the Preliminary Plan Worksheet, which follows the recommended action exercises. The advantage in completing this worksheet is that it shortens the time to prepare your Preliminary Plan and ensures that you consider all the necessary elements. Three sample Preliminary Plans are shown after the Preliminary Plan Worksheet.

Action Exercises

1. Write a Preliminary Plan for the presentation topic you have selected, following the Guidelines for Preparing a Preliminary Plan. You may wish to use the Preliminary Plan Worksheet. Concentrate in particular on Guideline 3, the main ideas or concepts. Be certain that your main ideas are stated as *conclusions* you want your audience to reach, and are not merely a list of subject areas. These statements should, in most cases, be complete sentences.

2. Ask some of your co-workers to give you feedback on your Preliminary Plan, particularly the main ideas. Find out whether the statements are clear to them; ask for their suggestions on clarification. See if they feel that your main ideas meet the criteria established in the guidelines and that these ideas will accomplish your objectives. Determine whether your co-workers approve of your choice of supporting factual information. Ask for recommendations. Don't feel, however, that you must justify your own approach. Reactions may be very helpful, but, ultimately, you're the one who has studied and given careful thought to the content. During your planning process, listen to their comments and use your own judgment about how much weight to give them.

Preliminary Plan Worksheet

Topic of the presentation: _____

Approximate date, time, and place for the presentation: _____

_____

Who asked for the presentation? _____

Presentation objectives (what will be the immediate results if this presentation is successful?):

1. _____

_____

2. _____

_____

3. _____

_____

4. _____

_____

Audience analysis (who are they, and what is their general knowledge of, interest in, and attitude toward the subject?):

_____

_____

_____

_____

_____

_____

_____

_____

_____

_____

_____

_____

Main ideas or concepts that the audience must comprehend and retain if you are to meet your presentation objectives:

1. _____

_____

_____

_____

_____

2. _____

_____

_____

_____

_____

3. _____

_____

_____

_____

_____

4. _____

_____

_____

_____

_____

5. _____

_____

_____

_____

_____

Factual information necessary to support the main ideas:

Main Idea 1 _____

_____

_____

_____

_____

Main Idea 2 _____

_____

_____

_____

_____

Main Idea 3 _____

_____

_____

_____

_____

Main Idea 4 _____

_____

_____

_____

_____

Main Idea 5 _____

_____

_____

_____

_____

Preliminary Plan: Example 1

Topic: Progress report on XYZ project.

Objectives:

1. To keep the customer informed regularly about the status of the XYZ project.
2. To communicate any problem areas and explain corrective measures being taken.

Audience: Customer's project director and related staff personnel. They are familiar with the project and will be interested primarily in the proposed delivery date.

Main Ideas:

1. XYZ project is currently eight weeks behind schedule, but we can bring it back on schedule with the following adjustments:
   - Elimination of a redundant testing procedure.
   - Minor change in product packaging.
2. We can keep our costs within budget if we can make these adjustments.
3. We can complete the project within three weeks if we make adjustments now.
4. We are meeting all performance standards.

Factual Supporting Information:

Main Idea 1—(XYZ project is currently eight weeks behind . . .)
   - Factors causing the delay.
   - Production changes being recommended.

Main Idea 2—(We can keep our costs . . .)
   - Detailed savings to be realized from production changes.

Main Idea 3—(We can complete the project . . .)
   - Detailed time estimates until project completion.

Main Idea 4—(We are meeting all performance standards.)
   - Key performance measurements.

Preliminary Plan: Example 2

Topic: Need for a new inventory control system.

Objectives:

1. To create an awareness of the need for the new system.
2. To gain management approval and support for the new system so that:
   - They will authorize the necessary funds.
   - They will authorize sufficient time for people to learn and implement the system.
   - They will approve implementation of the new system both verbally and in writing.

Audience: Top management plus other management personnel at director level or higher. Most will have a general knowledge of the subject. A few will be favorably inclined to acquire and install the recommended new system, but many will be neutral, skeptical, or slightly hostile.

Main Ideas:

1. Our current inventory control system is inadequate to meet current and future requirements.
2. A new system is essential if we are to survive in the industry.
3. Our customers will respond positively to the benefits of a new system.
4. Money invested in the new system will be returned manyfold in the future.
5. Time spent in orientation and training in the new system will result in a much more profitable use of time in the future.

Factual Supporting Information:

Main Idea 1—(Our current system is inadequate . . .)

   - Sales and profitability trends over past five years.
   - Records showing inaccurate and unaccounted-for inventory over the past five years.

- Increased delays in turnaround time due to breakdowns in current system.

Main Idea 2—(A new system is essential . . .)

- Industry trends.
- Benefits of new system.

Main Idea 3—(Our customers will respond . . .)

- Statements from current and former customers.
- Statements from field sales personnel.

Main Idea 4—(Money invested . . .)

- Projected cost of updating current system if retained.
- Projected cost of purchasing and installing new system.
- Projected annual savings, if any, from use of new system.
- Projected increased sales, if any, as a result of improved accuracy and delivery of primary and supporting products.

Main Idea 5—(Time spent . . .)

a. Estimated time required for orientation and training.
b. Impact on production as a result of training time.
- Projected annual savings of time, if any, from use of new system

Preliminary Plan: Example 3

Topic: Support role of financial departments

Objectives:

1. To explain the support functions of financial departments to line managers so they will . . .

- Recognize and use those services available to them.
- Accept guidance from financial staff members as desirable and helpful.
- Seek assistance before rather than after problems occur.
- Provide positive feedback that will enable the financial departments to improve their service.

Audience: Division line managers. Most will have limited knowledge of or interest in the functions of financial departments and will be neutral to slightly hostile.

Main Ideas:

1. Financial departments are in business to help make the line manager's job less complicated.

2. Financial departments make many useful services available to line managers in addition to the familiar routine operations (payroll, accounts receivable, accounts payable, and so on).

3. Personnel in financial departments are skilled professionals with a desire to help.

4. Early identification of potential problems can enable line managers to receive more useful and less costly assistance from financial departments.

5. Financial departments are seeking feedback on their service.

Factual supporting information:

Main Ideas 1 and 2—(. . . make line managers' job less complicated; . . . many useful services . . .)

- Brief identification of only those services of direct concern to this audience.

Main Idea 3—(. . . personnel are skilled professionals . . .)

- Specific examples of services that have been or could be provided—in terms of benefit to users (line managers).
- Brief identification of key staff members likely to relate to *this* audience.

Main Idea 4—(Early identification of potential problems . . .)

- Examples of positive consequences of early identification. (Avoid mentioning or minimize negative consequences of failure to identify potential problems early.)

Main Idea 5—(Financial departments are continually seeking feedback . . .)

- Examples of improvements made as a result of feedback.

▶ STEP 4: Select Your Resource Material

For most presentations, finding *enough* resource material to include is not difficult. Rather, the problem is selecting **what** and **how much** material you should include.

If you've done your homework on the first three steps, Step 4 becomes relatively easy. Instead of plowing through a mass of data, which may be your natural inclination, you can proceed in a much more focused manner. Now that you've reached this point, the next step is primarily applying common sense, asking yourself a series of logical questions as you determine what material you should include.

What Should You Include?

Preparing your Preliminary Plan is essential to effectively selecting your resource material. Ask yourself these questions.

1. What is the **object** or **purpose** of this presentation?
   Is it to be persuasive, explanatory, instructional, or a briefing? Do you want to arouse interest, test an idea, recommend action, inform, or resolve problems? (Review your objectives in your Preliminary Plan.)

2. What should you **cover**? What can you **eliminate**?
   Supporting factual information identified in your Preliminary Plan should indicate what subject matter you need to cover. If the items you have identified don't contribute significantly to the accomplishment of your presentation objectives, you should eliminate them.

3. What amount of **detail** do you need?
   The amount of detail depends on several factors: your preparation and presentation time, your audience and their particular interests, and how much your audience

must know in order for you to accomplish your presentation objectives. Most presentations we have observed include much more detail than necessary. It's far better to leave your audience a bit hungry—wanting more detail—than to give them so much that they get confused or bored. You may wish to have additional details available, in the event that you are asked for them, without including them in your presentation. You can always include them in a handout.

4. **What must you say** if you are to achieve your presentation objectives?

   The answer to this question depends on the main ideas you identified in your Preliminary Plan. You must decide what specific resource material is essential if your audience is to accept your main ideas.

5. What is the **best way for you to say it**?

   Primarily considering your audience, what types of subject matter and what method of presentation (examples, anecdotes, statistics, comparisons, and so forth) do you think will get your main ideas across?

6. What kind of **audience action** or **response** are you seeking in order to meet your objectives?

   Do you need to force an immediate response (such as approval of a plan or authorization of additional money)? Or should you provide food for thought that will establish a favorable climate for follow-up?

7. What material should you **withhold from your presentation** but have **available for reference** if required?

   Is there some information that isn't essential to your presentation objectives but that you should have in reserve in the event someone in your audience raises questions about the topic?

8. Finally, submit all your resource material to the "**Why?**" test. Try to look at the material you've selected objectively, as if you are a disinterested observer. Examine each item you've selected for inclusion in your presentation and ask your-

self, "Why should I use this? What contribution will it make to achieving my presentation objectives?" You should eliminate whatever cannot withstand this critical evaluation. Answering this question can be somewhat painful, because there is a natural tendency to include information that's especially interesting or meaningful to you. But, in reality, this information might hold very little interest for your audience and, worse, might dilute the ideas essential to accomplishing your presentation objectives.

Are these questions a magic formula for the proper selection of resource material? No! Do they involve the application of common sense? Yes! Your logical, careful analysis of material to include in your presentation, always with your audience and objectives in mind, is vital to your presentation coming across *loud and clear.*

Action Exercises

1. Using the topic you have selected, answer the questions on the worksheet, identifying in writing all resource material you will include in your presentation.
2. Have your co-workers review your selections. You should be able to justify the inclusion of each item, both to them and to yourself; otherwise, eliminate it.

Resource Material Worksheet

Complete the following questionnaire to select what and how much material should be included to effectively support your main ideas. This will ensure that you don't use too much or too little resource material. (Refer to page 42 for complete explanations.)

1. What is the object or purpose of this presentation?

_____

_____

2. What should you cover? What can you eliminate?

_____

_____

3. What amount of detail do you need?

_____

_____

4. What must you say if you are to reach your presentation objectives?

_____

_____

5. What is the best way to say it?

_____

_____

6. What kind of audience action or response are you seeking in order to meet your objectives?

_____

_____

7. What material should you withhold from your presentation but have available for reference if required?

_____

_____

8. Submit all your resource material to the "Why?" test.

_____

_____

Now make a list of all the resource material you will need to include in your presentation. Also make a list of additional material that you should have available for reference, if necessary.

_____

_____

_____

_____

_____

_____

_____

_____

_____

_____

_____

_____

_____

_____

_____

_____

_____

_____

_____

_____

▶ STEP 5: Organize Your Material

OK—now you can work on what you will say and when you will say it! You have selected your resource materials in line with your Preliminary Plan; now you must organize that material into an effective presentation that will reflect your abilities, convey your honest beliefs, meet your objectives, and satisfy the needs of your audience. This chapter will help you:

▲ Capitalize on the peak periods for audience retention during your presentation.

▲ Prepare a dynamite opening that sets the stage for a favorable reception of your message by your audience.

▲ Create a varied approach to presenting the main content of your presentation that will keep your audience focused on your message.

▲ Close your presentation with a thought-provoking summary and an appropriate call to action.

▲ Make certain that your message comes through *loud and clear.*

We will start by considering the characteristic changes in the level of audience attention *and retention* during the course of your presentation, which will strongly affect your choices of timing and emphasis. We will examine the opening, the main content, and the closing—the three major sections into which most presentations can be broken down. Each serves a very specific purpose and requires a distinct approach.

How Does Audience Retention Affect the Organization of Your Presentation?

What your audience remembers determines whether or not you achieve your presentation objectives, so you need to be aware that certain parts of a presentation are remembered better after the presentation is over. Look at the *audience retention curve* shown here. While many factors—such as time, room arrangement, predisposition of your audience, and so forth—will have an effect on this curve, it tells us something about how your audience will react to your presentation.

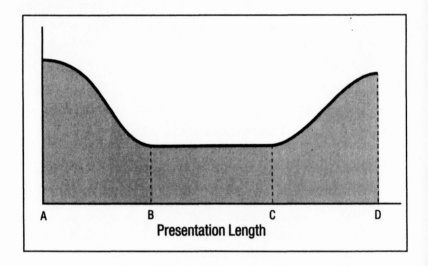

Curiosity will probably produce a reasonably high level of both attention and retention during your opening (A). Unfortunately, the retention level for a poor opening may be just as high as for a good one and may color your audience's attitude toward your entire presentation. Thus, it is doubly important for you to gain your audience's support during your opening.

Following your opening, you can expect a reasonably sharp drop in retention (B), even with a good presentation. Unless your content is very short and simple, a drop *will* occur, you can be sure of that. Naturally, the bottom of the curve is not as smooth as the illustration indicates. There will be peaks and valleys during the main content of your presentation. When you deliberately change your pace, tell a story, provide an illustration, or involve your audience during the main content of your presentation, you can help counteract this drop in retention.

Your effectiveness as a presenter will significantly influence the rise at the end of the curve (C). If you run out of things to say and simply stop, you may end your presentation with the retention curve at the low level indicated by Point C. If you run out of things to say and *don't* stop but ramble on with unnecessary repetition instead, the curve may drop off to nothing or, worse, it may rise, indicating that your audience will go away remembering your dull ending and thinking your entire presentation was a waste of time. However, if you use an appropriate summary statement to tip off your audience that your presentation is coming to a close, the retention curve will take an upward swing. You can then take advantage of this rise in attention to help those mental wanderers in your audience to get back on track and carry something of value away from your presentation (D).

What Makes a Dynamite OPENING?

Your opening has three powerful purposes.

1. The first, and perhaps most important, purpose is to *sell your audience on listening to your presentation.* Your opening is a particularly critical point in your presentation. Most audiences, as noted earlier, have a natural curiosity at the beginning. Whether or not your audience retains that curiosity or interest will depend, to a large extent, on your opening remarks and on how effectively you convince them that it will be worthwhile to listen to you attentively.

2. The second, and more obvious, purpose is to *introduce your subject* or the reason for your presentation. A simple, accurate statement is called for. This part of your opening should be interesting and *brief!*

3. The third purpose is to *establish your personal credibility* with your audience. Tell them why you are the one making the presentation. If another person is going to introduce you, give him or her information that will help establish your credibility.

> **Advantages of an Effective Opening**
>
> ▲ It creates a level of curiosity and expectation that results in a higher level of attention and retention.
> ▲ It satisfies your audience's WIIFM (What's In It For Me?).
> ▲ It sets the tone for the rest of your presentation.

Six Sample Openings

Here are six of the many different ways in which you might open a particular presentation. For illustration, we will use "The Need for a New Inventory Control System" once more as our topic.

1. **Direct statement** of the subject and why it is important to this audience.

   We're at a critical time in the life of our company. We have more intense competition than ever before. To remain competitive, we need faster, more accurate delivery of our primary and support products to our customers. Our current inventory control system, which is nearly ten years old, simply cannot meet that challenge. First, let me share with you some of the problems that are increasingly occurring. Then, I will offer some alternative ways of approaching these problems, together with the approach that our team believes has the greatest potential for meeting our future as well as our current requirements.

2. **Indirect opening** dealing with some *vital interest* of your audience and connecting your presentation objectives with that vital interest.

   As we are all painfully aware, our profit-sharing bonuses this year are likely to be at their lowest point in the past three years. There are two major contributing factors. The most obvious one is that our sales are significantly below our projections. A less obvious factor is that our inventory costs have skyrocketed. We believe these two factors are closely connected. We also believe that making an immediate investment in a new inventory control system will help increase sales NOW and decrease inventory costs in the future. Let me share with you how we reached this conclusion and what we firmly believe will change the direction of these two trends for the better, producing increased profits and increased profit-sharing bonuses.

3. **Vivid example** or comparison leading directly to the subject.

   Last month our company had to forgo bidding on a potential $10 million contract because our analysis showed that, under our present inventory control system, we couldn't meet the contract requirements for delivery of primary and support products. How many contracts like this can we afford to lose to our competition? Not one more! The time to act is NOW! This means investing in a new inventory control system that will ensure that we can take our place as one of the leading-edge companies in our industry. Let me show you how we reached this conclusion and what we believe will make this happen.

4. **Strong quotation** related to the subject that will be particularly meaningful to your audience.

   At our first annual meeting after we became a publicly held company, our founder stated, "We pride ourselves on being Number One in our industry in customer service. We intend to maintain that position for the foreseeable future." I wonder how many of our current customers would agree with the accuracy of that statement today in view of the unacceptable delays we have had in delivering our primary and support products. A major contributing factor to these delays has been an antiquated inventory control system that has been unable to respond effectively to our current customers' demands. We believe that investing in a new inventory control system NOW will go a long way toward helping us regain the position our founder committed us to. Let me show you why we believe that and what we can do about it.

5. **Important statistics** related to the subject.

Five years ago, our on-time delivery of our primary and support products to our customers exceeded 97 percent. Last year, for the first time in our history, our on-time delivery record was less than 90 percent. Five years ago, the number of repeat customers we had exceeded 65 percent. Last year, that number dropped below 50 percent. While there are many factors that contribute to these changes, we believe that one of the most significant factors is an inventory control system that can no longer meet the requirements of today's customers. Let me show you why we believe this is true and then present our recommendation for a new system that, we believe, will go a long way toward reversing that trend.

6. A **story** or **anecdote** illustrating the subject, provided it is directly relevant to the presentation and is not merely contrived for entertainment purposes.

*The other day I walked into a book store that had everything. A cappuccino bar; big comfy armchairs; beautiful music playing; a play area for kids; even a big section of CD-ROMs. I looked around the store and saw it was missing only one thing—*books! *Now that's a lesson for our current inventory control system. We've got excellent market research; we've got great salespeople—but we still won't make any sales if we can't find enough product to sell. There is a cure for this malady, however. A new inventory control system is just what the doctor ordered. Let me share with you what leads me to that conclusion.*

Naturally, you would select only one of these as your opener. Any one of these six types might be appropriate under one set of circumstances and inappropriate under another. Since the first image you project is vitally important in getting your audience's attention, you should open your presentation with whatever approach you can handle most effectively. Let's face it! You might not be a great storyteller. Therefore, opening with a story or an anecdote might be a poor choice for you. You need to select the approach that will work best for you, bearing in mind that you want to sell your audience on listening to your presentation as well as to introduce the subject and establish your own credibility.

How Can You Cover Your MAIN CONTENT without Putting Your Audience to Sleep?

Once you state your main ideas, you need to explain them in whatever detail is necessary to accomplish your presentation objectives. Often, your audience will look for patterns or relationships among the main points. You can develop your ideas by using:

- ▲ **A problem/solution approach.** Identify a problem and show how it can be resolved.
- ▲ **A cause/effect approach.** Show both negative and positive effects of specific actions.
- ▲ **A chronological approach.** Trace something historically, then project it into the future.

Or you can use any other method that will help your audience understand your subject and the points you want them to retain.

Your approach should highlight your audience's particular interest in the subject and should be fleshed out with examples likely to create a favorable or unfavorable response. The proper use of examples is so important that, if you must make a choice, it is usually better to eliminate some facts than to cut out examples of those facts that are more likely to help you accomplish your objectives.

Ten Ways to Make Your Main Content More Interesting

Here are ten keys to helping your audience learn. Some of these will be familiar to you; some may benefit from a brief explanation. Remember, it's not what's taught but what's caught!

1. **Develop analogies**, showing comparisons to similar but quite different factors. This is extremely important, particularly if you're presenting technical information to a nontechnical audience. For example, an article in a newspaper described the capabilities of the Hubble telescope. To make it more easily understood by people who might be unfamiliar with the telescope's technology, the writer described the surface precision of the mirror installed in the Hubble this way. *"If the mirror was as large as the United States, the bumps and pits in its surface would be less than two inches from top to bottom. As a comparison, if a standard eyeglass lens were changed to an equivalent size, its irregularities would show 500-foot mountains and valleys."* Presenting technical information in a way that your audience can relate to will help increase their understanding of that information.

2. **Use humor.** There are two benefits to using appropriate humor. First, when you relax, your audience relaxes, which allows them to be more receptive to your message. Second, significantly more learning takes place when accompanied by humor. What if you can't tell a joke well? Not many of us can. Not a problem! Look for incongruities or exaggerations, or perhaps create a cartoon illustrating your point (unless, of course, you know a key member of your audience dislikes cartoons). Using "The Need for a New Inventory Control System" example, a cartoon of an empty delivery truck with the driver asleep while waiting for products to be loaded might make a telling point while getting at least a smile from members of your audience. If you plan to tell stories or jokes, make sure they're relevant to your key point or topic and rehearse them in front of other people several times to make sure they work!

3. **Quote from current newspapers or magazines.** The more current your information, the more impressed your audience will be. Quoting a political figure, a well-known sci-

entist, or a sports hero who makes a statement that is relevant to one of your main ideas can make a tremendous impact on the audience. If you have a particularly appropriate headline from that day's newspaper, you might want to make a transparency of it that you can include in your presentation. There's lots of good material in newspapers and magazines that you can adapt to your message if you look through publications with that purpose in mind. To help you find interesting, noteworthy, and relevant material to illustrate your key points, at least 30 percent of what you read should be *outside* your area of expertise. Don't limit yourself to research documents and professional journals. You'll be surprised at what you can find in monthly magazines on the racks in your supermarket.

4. **Tell personal stories.** Stories that relate to your personal involvement in the project or the subject that you are presenting can create real interest. Using self-disclosure, including examples of where you may have made stupid errors, shows your vulnerability as well as your expertise. Audiences tend to relate better to presenters who do not try to set themselves up as perfect.

5. **Use examples and illustrations** describing your ideas in operation. These may include flowcharts, anecdotes, photographs, and anything else that might highlight your key points. As soon as you say the words *"for example . . . ,"* members of your audience will perk up and listen more attentively.

6. **Repeat** your main ideas in the same or different words to help summarize your points, drive them home, and ensure that your audience remembers them.

7. **Reinforce your ideas with relevant statistics.** Statistics can be very effective if you use them sparingly, present them as simply as possible, and support them with clear and powerful visuals. It's hard for your audience to argue with facts if they are backed up by convincing statistics.

8. **Display charts and graphs** that illustrate your key points. Make certain they are relevant to your message and easy to read.

9. **Draw on expert testimony** from users of the product or procedure who can provide credibility to your audience.

10. **Involve your audience.** You can do this by:

    - Asking questions of your audience and responding to questions from them.

    - Having them complete a worksheet or questionnaire.

    - Leading them in a brainstorming session regarding new ideas.

    - Calling on individual audience members to share their experiences (you may want to alert individuals in advance that you will call on them).

    - Inviting them to actually work with a product or process during your presentation.

The important key to remember is that adult audiences like to be involved with your presentation at some level. Most audiences do not like to be lectured to.

Remember this guideline:

▲ *If you tell me, I'll listen.*

▲ *If you show me, I'll pay attention.*

▲ *If you involve me, I'll learn.*

How Can You Make a Powerful CLOSING?

Try one of these phrases:

▲ *Now let's review the main points we've covered . . .*

▲ *To sum up these factors . . .*

▲ *Our primary purpose today has been to . . .*

▲ *My one last point before we close . . .*

Using such phrases makes it evident that you are going to wind things up. It will also help raise your audience's level of attention and retention (remember the Audience Retention Curve). Using such phrases tends to bring your audience back on target and gives you an opportunity to restate your main ideas, challenge your audience, summarize your major points, suggest agreement, or recommend action.

Another key to an effective closing is to integrate your opening points into your closing comments. This shows cohesiveness and ends your presentation powerfully. For example, *"What we've talked about in the past 30 minutes will have a direct impact on our operations in cost and efficiency as well as in service to our customers. As I mentioned in my opening statement, a new inventory control system is essential to our remaining competitive in today's marketplace. I believe that the system I proposed to you today will give our company the competitive edge we need."*

Any idea you want your audience to remember needs to be repeated *from three to ten times* during your presentation, either verbatim or expressed in different words with a slightly different slant. Repetition does not insult your audience, despite the common belief that it does. Obviously, you must exercise good judgment in using repetition, but you are naive, indeed, if you expect the majority of your audience to remember any point—even a significant one—if you make that point only once.

Advantages of Delivering a Convincing Closing

▲ A convincing closing brings your audience from a potentially low-attention state of mind into a high-attention and more receptive state of mind. As soon as you begin your closing, you'll have the majority of your audience's attention. They are now more likely to be receptive to what you have to say. Make it powerful and productive.

▲ A convincing closing allows you to summarize your main ideas, review the purpose of your presentation, and appeal for audience action. When you deliver a well-developed closing, you'll be much more likely to get the response you want.

▲ Your audience will leave feeling that attending your presentation was worth their time.

Four Closings That Will Impress Your Audience

1. **Challenge your audience.** For example, when you have presented a new process for handling customer inquiries, you may wish to close with a challenge such as . . .

   • *Can we be ready to implement this system within the next two months and thereby demonstrate to our customers and our competition that we deserve the label "Number One in Customer Service"?*

   • *Will you take the time to compare the two systems we've presented to you so you can decide for yourselves which system will give us the competitive edge we need? After all, we're depending on you to make this happen.*

2. **Summarize key points.** This is particularly effective when you are giving an informational or explanatory presentation and it's important to recap the main ideas to ensure understanding. For example:

   • *Whenever you have a system that goes down, it's important to remember the following steps . . .*

   • *In summary, let's review the four key steps necessary to make this program a reality.*

3. **Suggest an agreement or recommend specific action.**

   • *With your agreement to move forward today, we can have this system up and running within 90 days.*

   • *Now that you've heard our summaries, can we agree that it's necessary to adopt a more aggressive approach to our marketing efforts?*

4. Present a quote, facts, or statistics.

- *The current market of 10 million potential buyers of our products will grow to 30 million in the next five years. If we're serious about being a major player in that market, the time to aggressively expand our efforts is now.*

- *"We already HAD the technical skills necessary to achieve our quality goals. What we DIDN'T HAVE were better communication skills and trust." These words were spoken by the president and CEO of a promising multimillion-dollar company that ended up in bankruptcy. Let's not let this happen to us. We, too, have the technical skills to meet our quality goals. What we need are the necessary communication skills and trust to make this company competitive in today's marketplace. Let's begin by taking the steps we have covered today, to change this problem into a solution.*

(Note: if you normally invite your audience to ask questions at the conclusion of your presentation, *hold your closing summary until after the question period.* If you do, the last thing your audience will remember will be what you want them to remember, not a negative question or comment someone has raised just before your time is up.)

Since the closing tends to be the weakest segment of most presentations, it deserves as much planning as the rest of your presentation, if not more. Your closing can be relatively brief, but it should be vivid and to the point in terms of what you want your audience to carry away with them. And, it should be spoken with commitment and conviction.

There are three *nevers* in a closing. Never, never, never close by saying:

1. Well, I'm about out of time.

2. That's all I have to say.

3. I'm being told I need to stop now.

Always leave your audience with some kind of positive emotion (remember what you identified in your AAA). In effect, your closing should be a mini-presentation that captures your primary message. Remember, in order to make an impact with your closing, you must speak with commitment and conviction!

If you have satisfactorily completed the first four steps in your preparation, the effective organization of material in your presentation will be purposeful, and your objectives are much more likely to be achieved. Your presentation is organized into three parts:

1. **Your opening** sells your audience on listening to your presentation, introduces the subject, and establishes your personal credibility.

2. **Your main content** makes up the bulk of your presentation and provides the detail necessary for your audience to understand your message.

3. **Your closing** allows you to summarize your main ideas, review the purpose of your presentation, and appeal for audience action.

The Guidelines for Organizing Your Material and the Presentation Worksheet, both found at the end of Step 5, may help you organize your material. The worksheet provides a simple way to coordinate your time, content, and presentation methods within the scope of your objectives.

Use all the imagination at your command and keep your specific objectives in mind as you devise effective methods for presenting your material. If you do, your audience will leave feeling that your presentation came through *loud and clear* and that it was worth the time they spent with you.

Action Exercises

1. Using the topic you selected, organize the material for your presentation, following the Guidelines for Organizing Your Material and using the Presentation Worksheet. Prepare your outline in rough form so that you can change it if necessary.

2. Have your co-workers look over your worksheet, give you their reactions, and suggest ways to increase your presentation's effectiveness. Carefully consider their comments, but remember that it is *your* presentation and you should use the materials and approaches that will work best for you.

Guidelines for Organizing Your Material

Opening

Your opening has three powerful purposes:

1. Selling your audience on listening to your presentation.
2. Introducing your subject matter.
3. Establishing your personal credibility.

Suggested approaches for your opening include:

▲ **Direct statement** of your subject and why it is important to your audience.

▲ **Indirect opening** dealing with some vital interest of your audience that you can link to your subject.

▲ **Vivid example** or comparison leading directly to your subject.

▲ **Strong quotation** related to your subject.

▲ **Important statistics** related to your subject.

▲ **Story or anecdote** illustrating your subject.

Main Content

In order to confirm that your audience has a clear understanding of the information presented in the body of your presentation, remember:

▲ The appropriate sequence of your main ideas.

▲ Factual information that will support your main ideas.

▲ Ten suggested ways to make your presentation more interesting:

1. Analogies
2. Humor
3. Quotes
4. Personal stories
5. Examples and illustrations
6. Reiteration
7. Statistics
8. Charts and graphs
9. Expert testimony
10. Audience involvement

Closing

Your closing should be a mini-presentation in and of itself. It should paraphrase your opening statements to demonstrate cohesiveness. An effective closing should include one or more of the following:

▲ **Challenge** to your audience.

▲ **Summary** of your main ideas.

▲ Suggested **agreement or recommendation** for action.

▲ Powerful **quote or statistic** that directly relates to your topic.

▲ **Story or anecdote** that drives home the message you want your audience to carry away.

Presentation Worksheet

Presentation topic: _____

Presenter(s): _____

Date, time, place: _____

General Considerations

1. How will the room be arranged (seating, name cards, and so on)?

_____

_____

_____

2. How many people do you expect to attend? How and when will they be notified of the presentation?

_____

_____

_____

3. What presentation aids will be required? Will equipment be available at the presentation site or must someone transport it there?

_____

_____

_____

4. Will you use handouts? What arrangements do you have to make for them? How and when will they be distributed?

_____

_____

_____

5. How and when will you handle audience questions?

_____

_____

_____

Presentation Outline

Time allotted	Content*	Methods, aids, examples

* *Opening:* Sell your audience on listening, introduce the subject, establish personal credibility.

Main Content: Develop your main ideas.

Closing: Summarize content, appeal for action.

▶ STEP 6: Practice and Evaluate

It's a rare individual who can take even a well-prepared presentation and deliver it effectively on the first attempt. Most of us have had the experience of planning a presentation that looks good on paper, only to have it fall flat in the real world.

Here are some presentation pitfalls (probably corollaries of Murphy's Law) that turn up regularly:

▲ Your words don't flow as smoothly out loud as they did on paper.

▲ You lose track of where you are.

▲ You discover that handling your visuals interferes with the pacing of your presentation.

▲ You discover that you don't know as much about the subject matter as you thought you did.

▲ Someone in your audience asks a question you can't answer.

▲ Your audience appears cold and unresponsive.

▲ The physical location does not lend itself to the type of presentation you had planned.

Interestingly, sufficient practice will help you address all but the last two pitfalls. You can even anticipate and address the last two with some foresight during your planning, preparation, and practice.

Practice does not guarantee your success, nor will it make a good presentation out of a poorly prepared one. What practice *can* do is:

▲ Increase your self-confidence and poise, making your audience more willing to believe you.

▲ Reveal flaws or gaps in your material in time for you to make adjustments.

▲ Give you a working familiarity with your material so that your words come naturally and spontaneously.

▲ Help you use your visuals in a smoother, more coordinated manner, so that they will strengthen and support rather than interfere with your actual presentation.

▲ Help you identify and prepare to deal with potential problem areas.

What Are Some Surefire Methods of Practicing?

There are four primary methods of practicing your presentation. Any one, or a combination of all four, can pay tremendous dividends.

1. **Make the presentation aloud to yourself.** Go off by yourself with your notes and the visuals you will be using. Imagine that you're actually making your presentation in front of an audience. Get a feel for the flow of your material. Practice with your visuals. Identify any elements that need "polishing."

2. **Videotape your practice session.** Videotaping your presentation is one of the most desirable ways to practice an important presentation, and, during replay, you can really concentrate on the most important elements. Set up the video camera in the area where your audience would be. Adjust the lens to isolate the desired field of vision. Again, imagining that you are actually making your presentation, video-record your entire practice session, including use of any aids. You may wish to evaluate the recording immediately or view it at a later time. Remember that you are your own best critic! As you watch and listen from your audience's viewpoint, you may discover some things that need your additional attention. You may also wish to have some co-workers evaluate the videotape along with you.

3. **Audiotape your practice session.** Although it doesn't reproduce the full effect of your presentation, audiotaping

allows you to hear how you sound and to determine whether your ideas are coming across as you wish. Again, you may wish to listen to the tape immediately afterward, either alone or with co-workers, or replay the audiotape later.

4. **Try a dry-run session.** Have some co-workers, friends, or perhaps some representative members of your intended audience sit in on your practice session. Although it is frequently more difficult than the actual presentation, this rehearsal is probably the most effective way to try out your techniques, to make sure your ideas are getting across as you want, and to learn how to field questions on the subject. It's much better to flub a rehearsal than it is to fail at the real thing! Be certain to provide your dry-run audience with enough background information so that they can gear themselves to react with the knowledge, interest, and attitudes of your intended audience. You may wish to have your dry-run audience fill out the Presentation Evaluation Guide, at the end of this section, from the perspective of your true audience.

Your practice session may go smoothly, thereby confirming that your planning and preparation were effective. Then again, you may identify several elements that need additional work or even major modification. The key to successful practice is to make whatever changes you decide on as a result of your evaluation. The Presentation Evaluation Guide will help you keep tabs on each element of your presentation. Use it to make notes during your practice session, as well as to have your co-workers evaluate your presentation.

Practice makes perfect is a tired cliché and rather inappropriate in this context, because you are unlikely ever to make a letter-perfect presentation. On the other hand, *no practice spells disaster* may be a very realistic statement. The best-prepared presentation in the world can fail to achieve its objectives if it is not presented effectively. *Practice makes permanent* may be a more relevant state-

Surefire Methods of Practicing

▲ Make the presentation aloud to yourself.
▲ Videotape your practice session.
▲ Audiotape your practice session.
▲ Try a dry-run session.

ment, because it helps you fix your presentation approach indelibly in your mind at a much lower risk than during your actual presentation. Remember, if you want to make certain that your presentation comes through *loud and clear,* the preparation process is not complete until you have actually rehearsed it.

Action Exercises

1. Practice your presentation on your earlier topic, using as many of the suggested practice methods as practical.

2. Have co-workers evaluate your performance during a dry-run practice session, using the Presentation Evaluation Guide. (Or use the guide yourself to evaluate a recorded practice session.)

3. Make adjustments in your final presentation based on the results of your practice sessions.

Presentation Evaluation Guide

Topic: _____

Presenter: _____

Evaluator:_____

Content

OPENING

1. How well does the opening generate interest in the presentation?

☐ Outstanding ☐ Good ☐ Fair ☐ Weak

2. Is the purpose of the presentation made clear?

☐ Yes ☐ Somewhat ☐ No ☐ Not sure

Comments: _____

_____

_____

_____

MAIN CONTENT

1. Do the main ideas come through clearly?

☐ Yes ☐ Somewhat ☐ No ☐ Not sure

2. Are the supporting factual information and any accompanying illustrations:

Interesting? ☐ Yes ☐ Somewhat ☐ No

Varied? ☐ Yes ☐ Somewhat ☐ No

Directly related? ☐ Yes ☐ Somewhat ☐ No

3. Is the presentation appropriate for the intended audience?

☐ Yes ☐ Reasonably so ☐ No ☐ Not sure

Comments: _____

_____

_____

_____

CLOSING

1. Does the closing summarize the main ideas and purposes?

☐ Yes ☐ Somewhat ☐ No ☐ Not sure

2. How effective is the closing in encouraging action, belief, and/or understanding?

☐ Outstanding ☐ Good ☐ Fair ☐ Weak

Comments: _____

_____

_____

_____

GENERAL

1. How do you rate the content?

☐ Outstanding ☐ Good ☐ Fair ☐ Weak

2. Do you believe that the presentation objectives are likely to be achieved?

☐ Yes ☐ Probably ☐ No ☐ Not sure

Comments: _____

_____

_____

_____

Presentation Evaluation Guide (continued)

Delivery

VISUALS AND SUPPORT MATERIALS

1. Are the visuals and support materials suited to the topic and to the audience?

☐ Yes   ☐ Reasonably so   ☐ No

2. Are they visible to everyone and easy to follow?

☐ Yes   ☐ Reasonably so   ☐ No

3. How effective is the use of these materials?

☐ Outstanding   ☐ Good   ☐ Fair   ☐ Weak

Comments: _____

_____

_____

PRESENTATION TECHNIQUES

1. Confidence: Does the presenter appear to be in control of the situation?

☐ Yes   ☐ Reasonably so   ☐ No

2. Are posture and movements appropriate?

☐ Yes   ☐ Reasonably so   ☐ No

3. Are gestures effective?

☐ Good   ☐ Fair   ☐ Overdone   ☐ Ineffective

4. Is the presenter's relationship with the audience effective (for example, eye contact, audience interaction, responsiveness to questions)?

☐ Outstanding   ☐ Good   ☐ Fair   ☐ Weak

Comments: _____

_____

_____

_____

VOCAL TECHNIQUES (check all that apply)

1. How are the presenter's pitch and voice quality?

☐ Good ☐ Too high ☐ Too low

☐ Harsh ☐ Nasal ☐ Monotonous

2. How about rate and intensity?

☐ Good ☐ Too fast ☐ Too slow

☐ Too loud ☐ Too soft ☐ Monotonous

3. Does the presenter use the pause effectively?

☐ Yes ☐ Reasonably so ☐ No

4. Does the presenter effectively emphasize key words?

☐ Yes ☐ Reasonably so ☐ No

5. Does the presenter speak clearly and distinctly?

☐ Yes ☐ Reasonably so ☐ No

Comments: _____

_____

_____

_____

GENERAL

1. How do you rate the overall presentation?

☐ Outstanding ☐ Good ☐ Fair ☐ Weak

2. Make any additional comments you feel would be helpful.

_____

_____

_____

_____

_____

_____

_____

_____

Summary: Final Thoughts on Preparing Your Effective Presentation

Any presentation you decide is worth making clearly deserves your best effort. Only in this way can you be reasonably certain you will achieve your presentation objectives.

Key Points to Remember in Preparing Your Presentation

▲ **Define your objectives.** Your objectives should answer the questions, "Why am I making this presentation?" and "What do I want my audience to do or feel as a result of this presentation?" If you don't know where you are headed, you could be unpleasantly surprised by where you end up.

▲ **Analyze your audience.** A detailed analysis of your audience will disclose a variety of needs, interests, likes, and dislikes. Keep this valuable information uppermost in mind during your preparation process; it can help you design a tailor-made presentation with the greatest likelihood of communicating your message to this audience.

▲ **Prepare your preliminary plan.** This is a systematic way to identify and document all your relevant factors (objectives, data on your audience, main ideas, and factual supporting information). It keeps your efforts focused and guides the efforts of anyone who may be assisting you with the presentation.

▲ **Select appropriate resource materials.** Assess selected material for relevance, establish the degree of detail that will be necessary, and determine the best way to present your resource material in order to achieve your objectives. Remember *less is probably better.*

▲ **Organize your material for optimum delivery.** Your opening should not only outline the purpose of your presentation, but it should also sell your audience on your own credibility and on the value of listening to what you say. Satisfy your audience's WIIFM (What's In It For Me?). Your main content should explain the main ideas in your presentation with an appropriate degree of detail and in a way that is understandable and interesting. Design an effective closing that leaves your audience with a vivid message that you want them to remember, thus providing you with the desired results you are looking for.

▲ **Practice and evaluate your presentation.** This is the part of the preparation that you will be tempted to leave out. And yet, it is the part that will confirm your success. This is your opportunity to identify and remedy any flaws and to incorporate worthwhile improvements that you may have ` thought about during your practice session.

If you have followed these steps in your preparation carefully, you now have a presentation designed to help you achieve your objectives. The rest of this book will help you take your presentation to the next level and increase the probability that your message will come through *loud and clear.*

3

Developing and Using Presentation Visuals and Support Materials

After you have carefully gone through the six steps in preparing your presentation, you are now ready to deliver it to your audience. Right? *Wrong!* Of course, if you just happen to be a dynamic speaker, and if your message just happens to be particularly exciting, you might be able to get by without visuals and other presentation support materials. But if you're like most presenters, you'll find the success of your presentation greatly enhanced by using creative visual elements to support your message.

This chapter focuses on the most dynamic part of the presentation process: the part that is experiencing an incredibly sophisticated change every day. By the time this book is published, there will be even newer and more exciting ways of presenting your ideas than we are able to address here. If you have avoided new technology so far, in favor of "tried-and-true" presentation techniques that have always served you well, it's time to take another look. You don't need to be a "techno-whiz" to use technology. You just need to recognize that you can't escape it. You can use the same planning methods to assure complete success in a low-tech presentation as in a global multimedia extravaganza. It's just the tools that change.

Let's face the facts. Photographs, graphics, video footage, and sound all add meaning to words and numbers. We have already learned through experience that:

▲ **Overhead transparencies** jammed with text do not have as much impact as bulleted transparencies, which, in turn, do not have as much impact as graphic representations of concepts.

▲ A **line drawing** of a new product doesn't have the pizzazz of a full-color photograph.

▲ A **flipchart** does not work in an auditorium with a thousand people.

These discoveries were quite easy for most presenters; they make common sense! Integrating real technological advances into presentations is no different. Sure, we have to learn to use equipment, master complicated software programs, *and* deal with the inevitable glitches that pop up whenever you attempt to do something new in a presentation. However, the very nature of presentations is changing. Don't be left behind!

Still, you shouldn't panic or throw in the towel altogether just yet. The constant use of technology—electronic media—is still far from the norm in most presentations. Computers and software are used more often to *create* overhead transparencies, slides, and handouts than they are to *deliver* the presentations themselves. There are just too many differences among the presentation formats available to make their use widespread right now. But don't grow complacent, either. If you keep your head in the sand and think that the dusty viewgraphs you have used for so many presentations will always be *all* you need, you're in for a great surprise!

The coming wave—according to seers and sages in the computer industry—is for fully integrated packages of simple-to-use software that incorporates text, graphics, animation, sound—just about anything that supports what we know as a presentation. Here's what these packages will do:

▲ Many presentation programs already offer "Wizards," templates for commonly used visuals that enable raw data to be transformed into a chart or graph, clip art to be imported from a compact disc, or full-color overhead transparencies to be printed at the click of a mouse.

▲ They provide tips and techniques, brainstorming tools and idea generators, standardized backgrounds, million-color palettes, and the ability to transmit finished presentations over data networks to remote locations, where they can be reproduced and used exactly as developed and intended.

▲ They help you decide on an overall "style" for your presentation, structure the content for a certain time limit, decide on the type of output (black-and-white transparencies, color transparencies, slides, computer), and even print your handouts.

▲ They allow you to import previously developed visuals from existing presentations or "drag-and-drop" elements of presentations into new diagrams.

▲ Best of all, they force you to think through the six steps in the presentation planning process.

As you approach the design and use of visuals, bear in mind that you, the presenter, are still the star of the show. Your visuals are simply *aids*. Your knowledge, clear thinking, and confidence will always overshadow any visual. Conversely, no fancy visual will make up for a poor presenter!

Before you sit down to plan your visuals, consider whether all of the following factors are correct and feasible:

▲ It is practical to have everyone who needs to hear your message together at the same time in the same place.

▲ The cost of having someone attend your presentation is worth the direct cost as well as the lost productivity that comes from their being at your meeting and away from the job.

▲ The information you will incorporate into the visual media supporting your presentation is accurate and timely.

▲ The method of delivering information that you have chosen is the best for each individual in your audience.

▲ You are not integrating technology into your presentation simply because it's available in your organization and it needs to be used.

But, enough of this philosophizing; let's get to the bottom line!

How Will This Chapter Help You?

We have divided this chapter into three sections.

1. **Design Your Visuals** to provide maximum support for your message. This section will focus primarily on the use of graphics and how they can capture your audience's attention so that your message comes through *loud and clear.*

2. **Display Your Visuals** to reach your audience most effectively. Here we will tell you how to use common presentation methodologies, starting with some of the more sophisticated computerized approaches. Then we will move to more traditional overhead and slide projectors as well as video. Finally, we will touch briefly on using familiar tools such as the flipchart, whiteboard, and handouts.

3. **Practice! Practice! Practice!** This section will include techniques for making sure you are using the visuals and the equipment for optimum results.

We also include a set of Guidelines for Effective Use of Visuals and Support Materials, which can be a ready reference as well as a resource, listing a wide variety of visuals and support techniques that you can use in your presentation.

What this chapter will *not* do is instruct you in the specific use of software programs, equipment, or other strategies that an individual commercial presentation package may include. Rest assured, however, that the basic planning model described in this book will be the best support you could have for making sure your message comes through *loud and clear!*

▶ STEP 1: Design Your Visuals

In any presentation, there are usually only a few main ideas (the ones you identified in your Preliminary Plan) that you *must* communicate to your audience. By concentrating on these main ideas, you can develop mental images and identify concrete results you can achieve with a particular visual representation.

Let's say that your company is rolling out a new product. The product has been in development for some time, has been field-tested, and modifications have been made. It is now ready for a major advertising campaign to make it a competitor in the marketplace. As the Sales and Marketing Director, you will outline the marketing plan to your Regional Sales staff, who are located in eleven different countries. You will deliver your message during a satellite transmission beamed to each of the regional centers. You will share product pictures, sample brochures, a proposed television advertisement, and sales goals and projections with your staff.

Your product photographs, sample brochures, and videotaped advertisements are relatively straightforward. Professional photographers, graphic artists, and producers have prepared your materials. You plan to use them "as-is" to support your presentation. However, you want your sales and marketing staff to be motivated to meet demanding sales goals. How do you best represent these materials to support your presentation? The first thought that comes to mind is a bar chart, indicating specific sales goals to be achieved within certain timeframes. This is a relatively direct way of communicating your goals. It is easy to understand, it translates readily to a graphic format, and it can be prepared quickly. However, you consider the rest of your presentation to be pretty "slick." How can you spice up that bar chart? A number of possibilities are available to you. One of the primary options involves the use of color. Bright, contrasting colors demand attention. Technology helps you consider an even more dynamic possibility: animation. You can actually show the bars "growing" as time progresses.

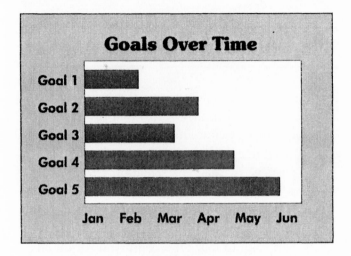

You can use representations of the product to replace the bars. You can even integrate sound, perhaps the theme song for the new ad campaign, into the background while you communicate your sales goals. Your "shoot for the moon" motivational campaign can include the sound of a rocket taking off, with goals colorfully highlighted below a picture of the moon. Suddenly, the creative possibilities are endless! While you will most likely need (and may already have) professional help to actually prepare such alternatives for a satellite transmission, just opening your mind to the number of possibilities that exist through using technology can

spur you to a more compelling and masterful presentation, even if you deliver it in your own conference room!

Holding your audience's attention is difficult when you ask them only to read from projected visuals. Consider these alternatives.

▲ **A list of statistics, per-centages, or sales projec-tions** is more appealing when it is presented . . .

Gross Sales	
1993	$ 10,296,228
1994	$ 12,424,309
1995	$ 13,693,040
1996	$ 13,986,522
1997	$ 14,300,000
	Projected

. . . as a bar graph or a pie chart.

▲ **Contrasting colors, shapes, or highlighted sections** can call attention to significant accomplish-ments.

▲ The **steps in a manufac-turing process** might be best represented in a flow chart.

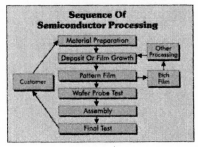

▲ **Icons** can substitute for words, product photos can precede a bulleted list of features, and clip art can easily add an element that clearly and succinctly helps to illustrate a concept.

▲ **Even text can come alive.** Using the animation features of presentation software packages, bulleted text can literally "sing and dance" its way into sight (perhaps using the theme from your new advertising campaign), or last year's model can be visually "morphed" into this year's model, highlighting noticeable changes.

While everyone might *like* to add such embellishments to their presentations, in the past they have often required more time and effort than many have been willing, or able, to invest. However, new presentation software programs have "point-and-click" features that can add:

▲ **Animation and sound effects,** textured backgrounds, text shadows, slide-to-slide transitions, or live action video.

▲ **Pre-arranged flowcharts,** timelines, 3-D effects, and organization charts.

▲ **Clip art libraries** that provide an array of graphics for quick insertion.

What Is Storyboarding?

One technique that allows a presentation message to be analyzed and translated into visual concepts involves the use of the *storyboard*. Long used in advertising, television, and film production, the storyboard involves simply listing key concepts and ideas and then portraying those concepts as visuals. While your finished visuals will probably be developed using presentation software, you may find it helpful to lay out your presentation manually, matching your proposed visuals to your content. You can list the key points in your presentation in a column on the left-hand side of a piece of paper. In a corresponding box in the right-hand column, draw a rough sketch of an image, describe what you would like, or attach a photo or clipping (hey, we can't all be artists!). Some presenters prefer to use index cards on which they write the main points and then sketch desired visuals. You can also develop the same process on your computer. Share your storyboards with

Key Concepts	Visual Representations
Welcome. Announce new profit levels. Establish need for further growth.	*Photo of headquarters building with words "Continued Success" overprinted.*
How company plans to engineer growth.	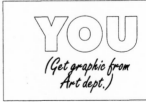
Percentage of revenue budgeted for new campaign.	

staff artists and photographers or with specialists who can assist in creating your visuals.

What Should You Illustrate in Your Presentation?

In every presentation, regardless of its specific content, there are certain key portions of your message that require illustration, particularly your opening and closing, as well as major ideas in your main content.

▲ **Opening.** You may want to start your presentation with a striking photograph, a cartoon related to your message, or a challenging question graphically displayed. The moment you present a visual stimulus, you will get your audience's attention. Therefore, make sure that your opening visual focuses on what you want your audience to think about first. You can use an appropriate graphic design or picture to personalize your initial visual for that specific audience. For example, you might have photographs of members of your audience in action or a graphic depiction of a startling contrast between where your organization has been and where it is headed.

▲ **Agenda.** Your second visual usually presents the agenda or goals of your presentation. It lets your audience know what to expect, and it shows that you have carefully organized and prepared what you are going to say. Use only key words or phrases, graphically displayed when possible. Fill in the detail out loud and, if appropriate, provide your audience with a handout. Don't clutter your visual. Keep it simple.

▲ **Key points.** Go directly to the main content of your presentation, again remember to use only key words or phrases, or—better yet—graphics, pictures, or other visual representations of the concepts you are presenting.

▲ **Closing.** Don't forget to close with a summary graphic that leaves your audience with a vivid image of the message you want them to retain.

Who Can Help You?

Our six-step planning model encourages collaboration in preparing effective presentations. In fact, in today's fast-paced and data-driven environments, few presentations represent the work of a single individual. Often, the development of a presentation (and even the presentation itself) is the responsibility of multiple team members. More organizations are recognizing that natural work groups or cross-functional teams from various disciplines (for example, marketing, manufacturing, finance, and operations) can create a presentation that is more likely to meet important objectives. At other times, a single individual may be given the primary task to develop a presentation while team members provide feedback and suggestions as the development proceeds.

For example, marketing people might provide product photos and brochures, engineers may have schematic drawings, lab technicians might have working prototypes you can use, and finance people could provide figures and statistics displayed creatively. Teams are often more creative than individuals, and their combined energy can also increase productivity. In addition, as team members work together in the development process, they learn from one another, assuring that the organization benefits from their combined knowledge.

What Are Some Effective Approaches for Arranging Visuals?

Naturally, you should arrange visuals to complement the type of presentation you are making (persuasive, explanatory, instructional, or briefing). Here are four commonly used arrangements that can help clarify your presentation: progressive disclosure, sequencing, serial slides, and question/answer slides. There are many others you may wish to explore as well.

1. **Progressive disclosure** is used most often when presenters display text and numbers. This approach allows your audience to see one thought at a time, followed by another, then another. To create this sequence, lay out the complete visual and then make a series of individual visuals, starting with one that shows only the first item, followed by another that has the first and second items, and so on. You can also use contrasting colors on succeeding frames. This way, your audience's attention focuses on the new thought that is disclosed. Changing the image as each new idea is presented also tends to stimulate your audience's interest.

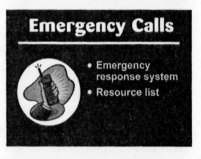

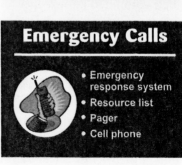

2. **Sequencing** is similar to progressive disclosure, but it involves pictures rather than text. A sequence of related visuals that develop a single concept is projected in building-block fashion. One example might be a simulated jigsaw puzzle that shows how the various elements of health and safety fit together. Another example could be the stages in the manufacture of a product, starting with design and engineering and ending with the finished product. Still another example of sequencing might be a pie chart with each slice projected in turn for individual consideration; then all the slices are joined together to represent the whole. Sequencing can strengthen your audience's comprehension of an idea.

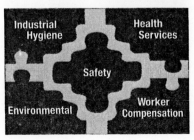

3. **Serial slides,** which compare several related items by showing them in a series, can also be a successful arrangement for your presentation. The evolution of a certain sail design in windsurfing over the years is a good example, as are *before, during,* and *after* shots of a construction site. Serial presentation also engages the full power and attention of your audience.

Sail Design
- Simple Design
- Triangle Cut
- Flat Cloth

Windsurfing 1982

Sail Design
- 3 Battens
- RF Design
- Strips Sewn to Add Air Pocket

Windsurfing 1988

Sail Design
- Fully Battened
- Camber Induced
- High-Tech Cut
- Mylar Material

Windsurfing 1997

4. Question/answer slides depict a direct relationship between the statement of a problem and its solution. A visual showing a question written out or a representation of some goal can focus your audience's attention on your point while you expand on it verbally. A subsequent visual can show the correct or desired answer. This technique is often used in interactive presentations, where the "question visual" generates audience involvement and the "answer visual" summarizes the discussion.

Where Do You Get Your Visuals?

With the widespread availability of computers and associated software, the use of graphic images has increased exponentially. They
are also easy to access and use in developing visuals without the
need for file cabinets filled with outlines, images, drawings, and
cartoons clipped from magazines, newspapers, company publications, and other published sources. These include:

▲ **Clip art libraries,** which require no royalties.

▲ **Computerized presentation programs** with integrated
graphics libraries, including drawings, graphics, symbols,
and so on.

▲ **Graphics software packages** containing a "drawing" capability that allows you to create or alter graphics.

▲ **Advanced packages** that allow you to make substantive
changes in your graphics, such as taking elements of visuals from several sources and melding them into something
completely original.

▲ **The World Wide Web,** which can access on-line "home
pages" of business groups, large corporations, and even
individuals. (Be aware of potential copyright issues when
you use graphics from such sources.)

Be cautious about using many of the more commonly found
graphics because they are *so* widespread that their impact may be
minimal.

Guidelines for Selecting and Designing Presentation Visuals

Key Concepts

An Effective Presentation Visual Must . . .

▲ Present an idea better than words alone.

▲ Represent one key concept (even though it may present a lot of information about the concept).

▲ Emphasize pictures or graphics rather than words wherever possible.

Visual Representations

The new model is far easier to use because of the following features: bigger buttons, wheels and battery power.

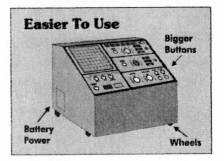

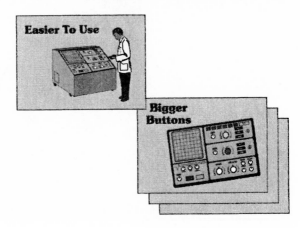

Key Concepts

Visual Representations

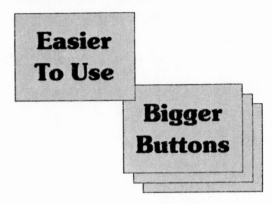

▲ *Generally restrict the use of text to a maximum of four words per line and six lines per visual, emphasizing short phrases or key words rather than complete sentences.*

▲ *Use appropriate color, font, and font size.*

Key Concepts

Visual Representations

▲ *Be carefully made: neat, clear, uncluttered.*

The most important thing to keep in mind about your presentation visual is that it should *support* your presentation, not be the center of attention. The content of your presentation should be able to stand on its own even if the electricity goes out or if your slides are sent to the wrong city. Presentation visuals should strengthen what you are saying, but they should require your interpretation. Otherwise, you become merely a robot that operates the machinery.

▶ STEP 2: Display Your Visuals

Now that you have carefully planned your presentation and selected the type of visuals that support your message, you need to decide the best way to display them. Will you show them with an overhead projector, use slides, print copies to use as a handout, or display them on a computer screen or LCD panel? Or is there another more appropriate method? Should you prepare both slides and handouts to reinforce your message?

Still Images

Overhead Projectors

The overhead projector, when used with conventional transparencies, is simple to operate and it offers you maximum control and flexibility as a presenter. It allows you to:

- ▲ Prepare your visuals using standard office equipment: computer, laser printer, or photocopier that puts images on transparency stock.
- ▲ Maintain eye contact with your audience while you still can read what you are projecting.
- ▲ Keep the lights up, retaining the rapport you've built with your audience and making it easier for anyone taking notes.
- ▲ Control your audience's attention by leaving the projector off until you are ready for them to see the image.
- ▲ Highlight a specific point on your transparency using a pen or pointer.
- ▲ Highlight the point you are making using color.
- ▲ Use a laser pointer (which can be seen with the lights on) from anywhere in the room.

Slide Projectors

Slides work extremely well when you are in a large room or auditorium and your visuals need to be projected to a larger size. Because slides maintain their resolution when they are enlarged, they serve very well for this purpose. They can be projected from the rear of the room or "rear-projected" from behind the screen. Either way, they present a superior image.

Also, a whole new generation of cameras has been born. Digital cameras take full advantage of computer capabilities, providing color, high resolution, and profound detail in the images they produce. Often, there is no film! Photographic images from line drawings to people or products are saved on computer disks. Images can be altered, refined, enhanced, adapted, and merged with other images using specialized software programs. While such imaging programs are not for "beginners," their utility will make including photographic images in presentations quite simple. Talk with your graphics department or service bureau about how to use this technology.

Of course, "regular" cameras are still readily available, with photographs capable of being used "as-is," or, with scanning capability, able to be enhanced with some extra steps. The crispness and professional image of slides tells your audience that your presentation has been carefully planned and well thought out.

How Do You Create Slides and Transparencies?

Earlier we mentioned that perhaps the most common role for the supercharged presentation software packages now available is to prepare visuals faster and simpler.

▲ **Using embedded visual templates,** you can type in titles and bullet points, and the software picks "default" point sizes and colors.

▲ You can **add clip art** from the library included with some programs or add it from libraries purchased or created for presentation support. This can be done with the click of a mouse. You can easily add and resize clip art, graphics, charts, and so on, to fit the proportions of the visual. Lines, arrows, dots, icons, and other symbols can be added with relative ease. Also, you can preview the draft visual to be sure that it meets your needs.

▲ **Scanners** allow you to copy photographs and even whole pages of text.

▲ **Large, clearly defined letters** and numbers and simple illustrations should be the rule in preparing transparencies.

▲ You should use **pictures or graphics** wherever possible. When text is essential, fill no more than half the viewing area.

▲ **Limit each slide to one idea.** It is better to use several simple slides than one complicated slide.

▲ **Vary the design** of each slide to avoid visual boredom or use clearly distinct titles so that the audience will immediately notice a change in content.

▲ **Use color for contrast** and to highlight important points.

There are many other tips for using various kinds of projection media that your audiovisual professional can provide or that are included in the Annotated Resources Appendix at the back of this book.

Video

In a society visually conditioned for motion, you may want to consider live action, when appropriate, in your presentation. More often than not, this live action will be captured as a videotape. The practical applications of video are limited only by your imagination and willingness to experiment. Here are some functions video is good for:

▲ Displaying complex or intricate maneuvers involving specialized equipment or extremely small components.

▲ Testimony from an expert, a consumer, or a top executive.

▲ When you want a sense of "being there" integrated into your motivational presentation (for example, a presentation about a sales contest with a prize of a complimentary weekend at a famous resort).

For presentations made to a large, geographically dispersed audience, videoconferencing—which allows simultaneous reception in locations across the continent or the globe—may be appropriate.

In short, there are so many new and evolving methodologies available that we could devote this entire book to them. Since that is not our primary purpose, we again recommend that you use the expertise of your audio-visual professional or the Annotated Resources Appendix in this book.

Low-Tech Presentation Support Materials

Although you may use overhead projectors, slide projectors, computer projectors, or video to support the vast majority of business and technical presentations, there are some low- and lower-tech items that can be beneficial to many presentations.

▲ The **whiteboard** (the modern-day version of the familiar classroom chalkboard) is one of the most useful, most available, and least-expensive types of presentation support tools that you can use. A whiteboard is often found in conference rooms that tout the latest presentation equipment, along with the special markers used to write on the boards and the common erasers used to erase them. Remember to use different colors. The contrast of the image on a white background makes your writing easy to see.

▲ The **reproducing whiteboard** is a high-tech version. Text or diagrams written on the reproducing whiteboard can become a hard copy with the touch of a button! These special boards can capture what is written on them, avoiding one of the most frustrating aspects of chalkboards or standard whiteboards: information, once erased, cannot be retrieved.

▲ The **flipchart** is a pad of paper mounted on an easel that offers some of the same advantages as the whiteboard. You can draw simple diagrams, key words, and outlines with ordinary marking pens and record responses from your audience during interactive sessions. The flipchart provides several distinct advantages over the whiteboard. There is no need to erase material written on a flipchart. A completed sheet can be simply "flipped over" to reveal a fresh sheet underneath or individual sheets can be detached from the pad and mounted on the wall for continued reference.

Whiteboards and flipcharts offer the presenter a number of advantages.

- **They are flexible** and provide plenty of space on which to display material (words, diagrams, sketches).

- They provide **a sense of immediacy**, giving your audience the feeling that this is the very latest information.

- They allow an idea, process, or design **to be progressively developed**, focusing your audience's attention on one step at a time.

- They provide a **feeling of spontaneity** and heighten audience involvement, showing that you are willing and able to immediately respond to their needs and interests.

▲ **Handouts or workbooks** also are an excellent source of presentation support. They can:

- Provide detailed technical information.

- Guide individual study and practice.

- Present administrative information such as objectives and evaluation procedures.

- Provide drawings, charts, and other information on hard copy to your audience, making their review and notetaking more personal.

Handouts are effective only if you give careful thought to their preparation and use. Here are some tips for increasing their effectiveness.

- Prepare a title for your handout.
- Use boxes, icons (pictures, symbols, and so on), and other graphic elements to direct your reader's attention.
- Emphasize key points by bolding, italicizing, underlining, capitalizing, or using various font sizes.
- Make ample use of white space for ease of reading.
- Use short, active sentences.
- Avoid unnecessary information.
- Vary your text using bullets, offsets, and other interesting layout designs.
- Consider making handouts of your most important slides to pass out at the end of your presentation.

▲ **Other Low-Tech Materials.** Here are some other materials you may want to consider to support your presentation.

- **Samples or specimens** to show the real object.
- **Models**
  - ▲ **Small-scale** to permit showing an entire operation without using large quantities of materials, to make a large operation visible, to show a project to be completed.
  - ▲ **Large-scale** to make an object large enough to permit handling, to identify small parts, to show internal operation.
- **Exhibits** to show finished products; demonstrate the results of good and poor practices; attract attention; arouse and hold interest; and adequately illustrate one .

idea (use light, motion, color, and contrast to help attract attention).

- **Worksheets** to provide your audience with hands-on experience in performing certain action; to provide a carryover to the job.
- **Manuals, pamphlets, instruction sheets, circular letters, outlines, and bulletins** to provide standard information and guidelines as well as reference and background material.
- **Cartoons, posters, and signs** to attract attention and arouse interest.
- **Photographs and textbook/magazine illustrations** to tie the discussion to actual situations and people, to illustrate the immediate relevance of the topic, or to show local activities.
- **Case studies** to tie together, for specific situations, the principles, practices, and procedures that are being explained, interpreted, or formulated by the group. It is much easier to visualize a procedure if you "Take the case of Company X . . ."
- **Examples and stories** to relieve monotony or tension, fix an idea, get attention, illustrate, or emphasize.
- **Demonstrations** to show how to carry out a suggested method or procedure.
- **Field trips** to present a subject in its natural setting, stimulate interest, blend theory with practical applications, and provide additional material for study.

Guidelines for Using Presentation Media

Visibility

▲ Can your presentation visuals be seen (and heard?) satisfactorily by everyone?

▲ Have you taken into consideration the size of the room, the number of people, proximity to a source of distracting noise, the seating arrangement, visual obstacles, lighting, and so forth?

▲ Have you brought overhead transparencies to use in a huge auditorium with hundreds in your audience? (A projected slide is probably the easiest and least-expensive alternative in this circumstance, though a computer-based presentation can also be projected with specialized equipment.)

▲ Have you followed the development guidelines discussed earlier and used an appropriate type size and properly contrasting colors?

▲ Is there so much information included on your visual that it just doesn't make sense for people who are not sitting close to the source?

Availability and Compatibility

▲ Will the equipment you need to use for displaying presentation visuals be available to you at the presentation site?

▲ Can it be made available at a cost (in terms of money, time, or convenience) that will not exceed its relative value to your presentation?

▲ Can you store the equipment out of sight of your audience before and after use to minimize distraction? A model of a particular piece of machinery, for example, can be effectively used, but it may distract the audience if it is left in view throughout the presentation.

▲ If you are using electronic equipment or a presentation software package, are they compatible? For example, if you are using an LCD (liquid crystal display) panel to project presentation visuals from a laptop computer, is the cable that connects the computer to the panel the correct one?

▲ Does your version of the software package that you used to develop your presentation, which you saved on a disk for portability, match the version available at the presentation site?

▲ Does the computer available at the presentation site support the software that you are using for your presentation?

There are so many options you need to consider when you display your visuals and other support materials that it is easy to become overwhelmed. Don't get carried away! Use common sense to determine the most effective way for you to present your message to *this audience* so it will come across *loud and clear.*

▶ STEP 3: Practice! Practice! Practice!

An all-too-common fault many presenters share is that they do not rehearse as much as they should. Our six-step model lists *practice* as one of the principal steps in preparing any presentation. Even if your content is top-notch, problems with the design of your presentation visuals or your handling of equipment could doom your presentation.

Practice allows you to be sure that you can operate any necessary equipment without difficulty. You can develop your ability to stand and move around naturally, without blocking a projected image. You can practice maintaining eye contact and rapport with your audience while you work with equipment or capture the audience's comments on a flipchart. In the final analysis, you will blend your content with your support materials to ensure that the materials and your handling of them enhance your presentation rather than compete with it.

We further recommend that you practice an important presentation at the actual location of your presentation, whenever possible, with the same equipment you plan to use during the real thing, and far enough in advance so that you can fix any major problems. Then if your equipment doesn't work, or a projected image can't be seen, or the room is more cavernous than you anticipated and you need a microphone, you can make the necessary adjustments for the success of your presentation.

A "dry run" at the actual site may disclose the following glitches:

▲ It is hard to see your projected images because you can't darken the room enough.

▲ The closest electrical outlet is too far from where you planned to locate the overhead projector.

▲ The meeting room setup has a fixed projection screen in an awkward location.

▲ The materials you shipped in advance have been locked in a storage room somewhere. You don't know where, and neither does anyone else!

▲ You discover that your computer was damaged in transit and will not allow you to access your presentation file.

▲ You find that you are fumbling with your materials because the lectern is slanted and there is no place for you to lay them out conveniently.

Seasoned presenters know that Murphy is alive and well and attends a large number of important presentations. Here are some more familiar examples:

▲ The extension cord for the projector is always a foot too short.

▲ The likelihood that someone will be out sick on the day of your presentation increases if that person has the only key to the equipment closet.

▲ You can plug some machines into all outlets, and all machines into some outlets, but you can't plug all machines into all outlets.

▲ People never throw away dried-out whiteboard markers or flipchart pens; they just leave them for the next presenter to try.

▲ Getting a sore throat the night before a presentation will guarantee that you have not arranged for a microphone.

Many presenters carry an "emergency kit" containing spare projection bulbs, electrical adapters, extension cords, batteries, and masking tape. If you are using a computer, a backup disk with a copy of your presentation can give you a measure of comfort if the original is damaged or lost. One of the most important items to include in such a kit is the telephone or pager number of an audio-visual specialist.

Ultimately, however, you should be able to present your ideas successfully even without visual support in the event Murphy takes over. If you follow the six-step model to develop the *content* of your presentation, you can accomplish just about anything.

In short, presentation visuals and support materials that have been ineffectively designed, that require frenzied last-minute improvisation, or that involve constant fumbling constitute incredible time-wasters and distractors. At best, such *preventable problems* will give a poor impression of you and the effort that you have made in preparing your presentation. At worst, they will keep you from achieving your presentation objectives.

Summary: Final Thoughts on Developing and Using Presentation Visuals and Support Materials

The purpose of any presentation is to communicate your message in such a way as to achieve *results.*

- ▲ Supporting your spoken remarks with visuals will markedly increase audience retention of your primary message—if you design the supporting materials effectively and use them skillfully.

- ▲ Technology is precipitating changes in the way that presentations are delivered. In fact, the very nature of presentations is changing because of technological innovations.

- ▲ The basic six-step planning model is still your best bet for ensuring that your presentations accomplish your objectives.

- ▲ Designing and preparing your visuals and support materials is basically a matter of breaking your message down into key points (which shouldn't be difficult once you've prepared your Preliminary Plan) and deciding how to illustrate each point convincingly.

▲ Storyboarding enables you to systematically analyze the content of your entire presentation and convert it into a series of accompanying visuals.

▲ These visuals should be clear and appropriate, focus on the current topic, and not be too numerous for your presentation's length. Most importantly, they should serve an auxiliary function (supporting rather than overshadowing your content).

▲ Whatever means you use to support your presentation, be certain those means are clearly visible or audible, that you can handle them comfortably, and that they are available at the presentation site and compatible with equipment or techniques that you plan to use.

▲ There is a variety of presentation support materials you can use, ranging from the lowest of low-tech (such as handouts or flipcharts) to the highest of high-tech (such as multimedia).

▲ Regardless of how simple your visuals and support materials are, there is no substitute for practicing in advance. Such practice identifies problems and glitches and enables you to prepare preventive measures.

▲ The fundamental principle governing the use of visuals and support materials is never to lose sight of the fact that, as their name suggests, they play a primarily *auxiliary* role. They support, *but are not replacements for,* a well-prepared and well-delivered presentation that comes across *loud and clear.*

Action Exercises

1. Thoroughly analyze the presentation you are planning, considering the types of visuals and support materials that we have discussed in this chapter. Select at least two differ-

ent types of materials and justify why they would most aid the accomplishment of your presentation objectives. Discuss your choices with your colleagues, incorporating any suggestions they might make, as appropriate.

2. Prepare a storyboard for a presentation that you plan to make, identifying your key points and concepts and suggesting appropriate visual representations for those points. Show them to your fellow workers to see how effectively they communicate the main points of your presentation.

3. Sit in on a presentation that uses a high-tech approach. Assess the visuals and support materials and the way the presenter uses them. Consider how you might use this approach in your presentations. Prepare a personal developmental plan that will help you gain and practice the skills necessary to become more comfortable with appropriate technology.

4. Expand the list of potential pitfalls that can mar a presentation or that are a part of your personal presentation experience. Prepare an action plan to help ensure that you do not repeat these problems.

5. Identify resources that will help you prepare your presentations. You can locate clip-art libraries (either hard copy or high-tech), photos, line art, or other graphic ideas to support the themes of presentations you are likely to prepare. Identify good ideas and make a note of them for your presentation files.

6. Use the Guidelines for the Effective Use of Visuals and Support Materials and Selected Types of Visuals and Support Techniques at the end of this chapter as ongoing reminders.

Guidelines for the Effective Use of Visuals and Support Materials

▲ Never use visuals or support materials in front of an audience until you have rehearsed with them.

• Be sure you know how to set up the required equipment properly (or have specialists who can do this for you) and that you know how to use it.

• Practice using your materials. Videotape your practice sessions and critique the videotape, or ask colleagues to provide feedback on your practice session.

▲ Make certain your visuals and support materials are a help rather than a hindrance to your communication.

• Design materials that are simple, clear, and represent facts accurately.

• Demonstrate only one key concept or idea per visual and be sure that the visual conveys the idea or concept better than words alone could.

• Keep the text to a minimum, emphasizing pictures and graphics instead.

• Use appropriate fonts, sizes, colors, contrasts, or other techniques to emphasize or clarify your main points.

▲ Don't waste your audience's time or cause audience distraction with your materials.

• Be sure all necessary equipment, components, and materials are available at the start of your presentation.

• Arrange the components of your presentation in the proper sequence prior to your session.

• Set up and adjust the equipment (or have it done for you) before your audience arrives; ensure that visuals and other support materials can be seen and heard from all locations at the presentation site.

- Wait until after you complete your presentation and your audience leaves before you pack up your presentation materials.

▲ Project! Speak with more volume than you normally require.

- Remember that your audience's attention is divided between you and the materials you are using to support your spoken words.

- Remember, too, that when you speak in a darkened room, you need more volume to hold your audience's attention.

▲ Don't stand between your audience and a projected image.

- Check to make sure that you aren't part of the projected image!

- Use a pointer to call attention to specific elements of a visual.

▲ Don't let your visuals or support materials distract *you*.

- Face and talk to your audience, not the projected visual.

- Don't interrupt your speaking pace when you change visuals.

- Use visuals and support materials to *support* your message. Avoid modifying your message so that you can use some "neat" technique.

▲ Don't let your visuals or support materials distract your *audience*.

- Don't project a visual until you are ready for it to be seen.

- Use visuals or support materials only when you make direct reference to them.

- When you finish using the materials, turn off the projector or cover up any models. Make sure your audience is paying attention to you and your message.

- Avoid passing items around during your presentation. Either show the objects to the group as a whole or display them after the session.

Selected Types of Visuals and Support Techniques

Here are several types of presentation support materials that you can use to make your topic easier to understand and more interesting, or to promote the kind of thinking that will help you accomplish your presentation objectives.

▲ **Charts. Use charts to direct the audience's thinking; to clarify a specific point; to summarize; or to show trends, relationships, and comparisons.**

Prepare information charts or tabulations in advance to ensure that you cover all points and that the information is accurate. Here are some of the more common types of charts:

Highlight	To present straight copy or emphasize key points.
Time Sequence (historical)	To show relationships over a period of time; may be used in any time unit, from seconds to centuries; can use pictures or graphs.
Organizational	To indicate relationships between individuals, departments, sections, or jobs.
Cause and Effect	To illustrate impact.
Flowchart	To show the relation of parts to the finished whole or to the direction of the movement. A PERT (program evaluation and review technique) chart is a flowchart.
Inventory	To show a picture of an object, with its parts identified, off to the side.
Dissection	To present enlarged, transparent, or cutaway views of an object.

Diagrammatic, Schematic, or Symbolic	To provide a simplified portrayal of naturally complex objects by means of symbols (for example, a wiring diagram).
Multibar	To represent comparable items using horizontal or vertical bars.
Divided-Bar	To show the relation of parts to the whole using a single bar divided into parts by lines.
Line	To display information using a horizontal scale (abscissa) and a vertical scale (ordinate); for example, showing profit increases/decreases over time.
Divided Circle or Pie	Used in the same way as the divided-bar chart.
Pictograph	To represent comparable quantities of a given item through the use of pictorial symbols (such as stacks of coins) representing comparable costs of different phases of an operation.

▲ Illustrations, diagrams, and maps.

▲ Videotapes or motion pictures (films).

▲ Slides.

▲ Samples or specimens.

▲ Models.

▲ Exhibits.

▲ Worksheets.

▲ Manuals, pamphlets, instruction sheets, circular letters, outlines, and bulletins.

▲ Cartoons, posters, and signs.

▲ Photographs and textbook/magazine illustrations.

▲ Case studies.

▲ Examples and stories.

· ▲ Demonstrations.

▲ Field trips.

CHAPTER

4

Delivering Your Presentation

Although this book primarily deals with preparing your presentation, the actual delivery is your "moment of truth." When you deliver your presentation, there are a number of specific techniques you can use that will have a significant impact on getting your message across. Here, we will focus on:

▲ **The nature of communication.** Exactly what is involved in delivering your message so that your listener will comprehend it.

▲ **Conquering fear of speaking.** How to get those butterflies flying in formation.

▲ **Presentation techniques.** How to make the best use of eye contact, appearance, gestures, body movements and facial expressions, and how to avoid distracting mannerisms.

▲ **Vocal techniques.** How to improve your pitch or inflection, voice quality, intensity, and speaking rate as well as such voice-related pitfalls as repeated use of "uh" and "um," voice drop, faulty pronunciation, poor enunciation, and speaking in a monotone.

▲ **Presentation tools,** such as the lectern and pointer. How to use them so they support, not detract from, meeting your presentation objectives.

▲ **Handling audience questions.** How to ensure this enhances and does not distract from your overall message.

What Is the Nature of Communication?

Isn't it amazing how shortsighted many audiences are? They just don't see your topic in the same way you do! Some audiences are like that, though, and you must learn to deal with them on that basis. And how do you do that? By *communicating* your message. (Come to think of it, if audiences weren't like that, there would be very little need for presentations. There might even be very little need for your services—a disturbing thought!)

To communicate your message successfully, you must realize that communication is a two-way process. Receiver/audience-focused communication requires more than just the transfer of meaning; it requires you, the sender, to *create* meaning. You achieve this by presenting your message so that it is simple for your audience to understand. You can do this with charts, graphs, examples, and other ways that we discussed in Chapters 2 and 3. This will increase the probability that your audience understands your message *exactly* as you want it understood. Using two-way communication reduces the possibility of misunderstanding.

Feedback is essential to test your audience's understanding and acceptance of your ideas. You can receive feedback, both positive and negative, in many ways—directly, by questions and comments by your listeners, and indirectly, by observing their nodding heads, facial expressions, vacant stares, attention and interaction, or the lack thereof. Inherent in all of these is a sensitivity on your part, an awareness of your listeners' reactions.

Too often, though, presenters make this mistake:

COMM NICATIONS

They leave the *YOU* out of communications, forgetting that the listener is the most important component in the process. For maximum impact, your entire presentation must be listener-oriented—prepared and delivered in a way that is understandable, interesting, and meaningful *from the viewpoint of your listener.*

How Do You Overcome the Fear of Speaking?

Bill Gove, the first president of the National Speakers Association, once commented facetiously, "I don't know why they call it stage fright. It's the *audience* I'm afraid of." This applies to many of us. The fear of speaking in public is considered to be the Number One fear in our society. It is feared more than death! Even though we've not heard of anyone dying while giving a speech, you may wish you had your obituary written before you speak your first word.

Lack of effective preparation and organization of your presentation can be one of your major causes of anxiety. The first three chapters of this book will help you prepare and organize your presentation so thoroughly that, with practice, you will gain the confidence you need to present your message in a calm, organized, well-disciplined manner. Here are six proven methods that may help you overcome any fear of speaking.

1. **Analyze your audience.** Complete the Audience Analysis Audit (Chapter 2) to make certain that your content is addressing the needs and wants of your audience. Most audiences will be more receptive if they feel you have their needs in mind, and, consequently, you will feel more confident about the reception your audience will give to your message.

2. **Conduct an individual audience survey.** Get to know some of the members of your audience personally, if you don't know them already. Call a few people ahead of time and ask some questions about your presentation. For example, if you're following up your presentation on a product your company has recently sold to this audience, asking front-end questions such as, "What's the greatest challenge you're having using this product?" or, "What is the product doing for you now that you weren't able to do before?" When you mention specific individuals by name and their comments, your audience will be impressed that you took the time to do this analysis and build their responses into your presentation. This is a level of tailoring that will make you look good and feel confident. Having made a connection with a few audience members ahead of time may turn them into your allies rather than potential enemies.

3. **Prepare for likely questions.** We tend to fear the unknown. When you rehearse your presentation in front of friends or colleagues, ask them to pose challenging questions. Prepare to respond to questions such as those during your actual presentation. If you know there will be some people in your audience who know more (or think they know more) than you do, try to make them your allies as soon as possible by talking to them ahead of time or by asking for their opinions during your presentation. Don't give them a chance to challenge or dispute your facts.

4. **Complete and review the various guidelines and work-sheets introduced throughout this book.** When you know that you have taken care of all details, you won't have these concerns distracting you.

5. **Visualize yourself giving a successful presentation.** Find a quiet place, close your eyes, and visualize your presentation from the time you're being introduced until the time you finish. Picture yourself standing in front of your audience, making a positive connection with friendly, familiar faces that make you feel comfortable. Hear yourself begin your

---

Ways to Reduce Fear of Speaking

▲ Analyze your audience.
▲ Survey your audience.
▲ Prepare for likely questions.
▲ Review guidelines and worksheets.
▲ Visualize a successful presentation.
▲ Prepare yourself physically and mentally.

---

opening words in a confident and assured voice. Continue to picture yourself moving through your presentation successfully, using your visuals, handling questions, and closing your presentation in a confident and positive manner. This is a powerful way to keep your thoughts on a positive note and not dwell on all the *what-ifs* that may keep creeping into your mind.

6. **Prepare yourself physically and mentally.**

   ▲ **Before your presentation:**

   - **Eat a light meal; avoid caffeine and carbonated beverages.**

   - **Arrive as early as possible** to become comfortable with the room setup and equipment and to introduce yourself to people as they arrive.

   - **Identify a key person to help you if necessary.**

   ▲ **During your presentation:**

   - **Memorize and rehearse your opening statement** to help you get off to a good start. This is the only part of your presentation we recommend memorizing word for word.

   - **Reduce or eliminate a shaky or cracking voice.** Here are three techniques that will help you.

   (1) Lower your pitch. Both men and women have a tendency to raise the pitch of their voices when they are nervous or angry. This causes your vocal

chords to vibrate in a range that lacks strength, resulting in a shaky or cracking sound to your voice.

(2) Tighten your stomach muscles. This is where your energy for your voice comes from.

(3) Increase your volume and push through the shaking or cracking. When we give in to nervousness, our voices crack and shake. Always feel your voice coming from your diaphragm, not your throat.

- Remember to breathe before and during your presentation. This may sound like a ridiculous statement, but many people say they forget to breathe while they are speaking and find themselves gasping for breath or without enough breath to complete a sentence. Just before your presentation, take a deep breath in and think to yourself, "I am"; then exhale and think "relaxed." Breathe evenly and rhythmically, not in sharp staccato inhalations and exhalations.

The best way to overcome the fear of speaking and control your butterflies is to plan, prepare, and practice, practice, practice! Remember, *practice makes permanent!*

What Presentation Techniques Will Help You Present Your Message Better?

Presentation techniques involve your nonverbal communication with your audience—how you use your body to support your intended message. How you use or misuse such elements as eye contact, appearance, gestures, body movements, and facial expressions has a significant effect on your listeners, and it frequently makes the difference between audience apathy and enthusiastic acceptance of your ideas.

Eye Contact

A vital part of effective communication is good eye contact. If you are an inexperienced presenter, maintaining eye contact with members of your audience can be difficult and frightening. It is a lot more comfortable to pick out a nice, inanimate spot on the back wall and speak to it or address your presentation to the screen where your visuals are being displayed! However, if you take the easy way, you will lose out on one of the most valuable resources available for determining whether or not your message is getting across—visual feedback.

Besides, your audience will have more confidence in you if you look them in the eye when you're making your presentation. Eye contact helps you establish a personal relationship with *each listener*. In addition, looking at a member of your audience, without staring, can be a very effective way of holding that person's attention or regaining it if it has wandered. (A comfortable time to retain eye contact with an individual is about three to five seconds.)

One very effective approach to maintaining uniform and balanced eye contact is to pick out several friendly faces in your audience, making certain that you select one from each section of the room, and then, if necessary, address your presentation to those individuals, shifting your eyes at appropriate intervals. The effect is that you are speaking directly to them and to their section of the room during part of your presentation.

Appearance

The confident presenter is one who looks assured, relaxed, and capable of doing whatever the situation may call for. Through experience, you can learn to give this impression, even when you're feeling insecure, by paying attention to a few rather important details.

▲ Dress in good taste with clothes that are clean, comfortable, and appropriate for the occasion. If informal dress is called for, use it. In more formal situations, avoid removing your suit jacket, loosening your tie, or rolling up your sleeves unless it is a working session and you want to set a mood. Use the information you gathered from your Audience Analysis Audit to help you select proper clothing and accessories, keeping in mind the image you want this particular audience to have of you and what you represent.

▲ Approach the speaker's area in the room in a deliberate and unhurried manner. Pause for a few moments after you get into position, smile comfortably, and look your audience over briefly before you begin to speak. This gives your audience a chance to focus on you, and it conveys the impression that they don't frighten you (even if they do!). Also, a moment of silence will normally do much more to attract your audience's attention than to launch into your presentation immediately.

▲ Whether you are standing, sitting, or walking, your posture should be relaxed without being sloppy, and dignified without being stiff, establishing the type of impression you want to make.

Gestures

"What do I do with my hands?" is a frequent question of the less-experienced presenter. Very simply, you should do what feels most comfortable to you or what seems most natural for you. If you're unsure, pay attention to how you use your hands when talking in an easy social situation.

▲ Hold your hands loosely at your sides; raise one to your waist; put one hand in your pocket, or even both hands if you can do it without looking too casual. (Be careful not to jingle coins or keys in your pockets.)

▲ Fold your hands loosely in front of you, rest them on the lectern, or hold your notes in them.

▲ Use your hands in a relaxed manner, one that does not draw attention to them at the expense of your message.

▲ And above all, avoid keeping your hands aimlessly in motion.

Your hands can also enhance your presentation. Well-selected and well-timed hand gestures can effectively promote the kind of audience reaction you want. Here are some of the more common types of gestures and the meaning they are likely to convey:

▲ *Sweeping hand* illustrates covering a broad field, takes in your entire audience.

▲ *Vertical or chopping motion* emphasizes precise points and breaks an idea into parts. (Avoid waggling your index finger, though, unless you intend to scold your audience.)

▲ *Palms out* says, "Stop!" or rejects an idea.

▲ *Palms up* invites acceptance, open-mindedness, or participation.

▲ *Upturned fist* can draw the audience to you and give aggressive emphasis.

In using gestures, keep in mind:

▲ Gestures must be appropriate to the impression you want to create. The wrong gesture is worse than none at all.

▲ They should draw attention to your idea, not to the gesture itself.

▲ Vary the gestures you use. If you overuse one, it loses its effect.

▲ Properly synchronizing a gesture with the word or phrase it supports is vital.

▲ Using too many gestures limits their value. Control yourself if you have this tendency.

Experiment with using gestures and rehearse them *in private* until they become comfortable. Although you may feel awkward at first, you will become more natural with gestures by practicing. Do not try out new gestures in an actual presentation (dry runs are OK) until you are reasonably confident about using them.

Body Movements

Occasionally using full-body movement during your presentation may serve your purpose. While pacing back and forth is certainly no help, deliberate, well-timed body movements help by:

▲ Relieving your tension.

▲ Drawing attention away from visuals and back to you.

▲ Breaking the hypnotic effect that standing in one place has on your audience.

▲ Changing the mood or pace of your presentation.

Facial Expressions

Your face, in particular, should reflect the mood you want to create in your audience. The deadpan presenter will not inspire interest or enthusiasm. In almost any presentation, the following facial expressions will be appropriate at one time or another: *serious, smiling, laughing, inquiring, doubtful.* Facial expressions should be lively, varied, and appropriate to you and your message.

Distracting Mannerisms

Many people have distracting mannerisms of which they are totally unaware. *Lip licking, nose patting, ear tugging, scratching, eyebrow fluttering,* and *head bobbing* are only a few. These mannerisms can fascinate, amuse, or repel your audience, and, in so doing, can prevent you from achieving your objectives. You can find out whether you have any of these mannerisms by asking a sympathetic, honest co-worker or by carefully reviewing a videotaped practice session. Becoming aware of the problem is half the battle. After that, it's up to you to do something about it.

Be natural! Don't try to be someone you aren't. Your use of nonverbal communication must be comfortable and appropriate to you, to your audience, and to your presentation topic.

What Vocal Techniques Will Enhance Your Presentation?

We have all encountered a speaker who presented interesting material and who used good presentation techniques but who either irritated us or put us to sleep with an unpleasant or monotonous voice. Worse still is a speaker you either cannot hear or cannot understand. You feel that your time is being wasted and whatever he or she is mumbling about probably isn't worth much anyway.

Very few people are endowed with the voice and oratorical ability of a Martin Luther King, Margaret Thatcher, Billy Graham, or Barbara Jordan. Most presenters, however, can substantially increase their effectiveness in using whatever vocal tools they have if they pay careful attention to certain basic elements of speaking and if they practice. Video- or audiotaping practice sessions can also pay rich dividends.

To improve your delivery, be aware of, and learn to control, the follow elements of speech:

▲ **Pitch or inflection** refers to your tone of voice. You should strive to maintain a conversational tone that is neither too high nor too low. The tone should be natural to you and you should vary it to prevent monotony. A pitch different from your normal speaking voice usually betrays nervousness and is distracting to your audience, particularly if they are familiar your conversational voice.

▲ **Intensity** is the force or loudness with which you project your voice. Depending on the size of your audience and the room arrangement, you should usually speak louder than you would in normal conversation. Your volume should be loud enough for everyone to hear you but not so loud as to overpower your audience. Variations in intensity can create a dynamic effect. At times, for example, a soft voice can command more attention than a loud one. If you lower your volume, however, you need to speak somewhat more slowly.

▲ **Rate**, or tempo, of speech is another important factor. The presenter who comes across like a machine gunner usually loses an audience almost immediately, because it is impossible for them to catch everything he or she says. The slow talker loses audience attention almost as quickly because every phrase is so drawn out and is boring or irritating. Again, taping your practice session can be a very helpful way to examine how good your timing is. Variations in rate can add considerably to the effectiveness of your presentation, provided they are consistent with the kind of mood you are trying to create.

▲ The **pause** is closely related to rate, and it can draw attention to points you consider particularly important. The strategically placed pause is a powerful way to stress a key idea you want your audience to remember. If you have a rapid rate of speech, the pause is an excellent way to allow you to continue with your rapid rate *and* give your audience some time to assimilate what you've just said. Use the pause deliberately, though, so as not to give the impression that you are groping for words.

▲ **Emphasizing** your key words, phrases, and ideas is an effective way to bring expressiveness to your voice and reduce its monotony, if that's your concern. Take the simple question, "How can I help you?" Repeat the question five times, one time for each word. Each time you say the sentence, emphasize a different word by increasing your loudness, changing your pitch and vocal intensity (either louder or softer). Pay attention to the different meaning each repetition sends to the listener.

Overcoming Vocal Problems

Here are a few of the more common vocal problems that can really trip up your delivery.

▲ "Uh" or "um" has long been the nemesis of public speakers. Such sounds occur most often when our thought processes interfere with our speech. We fail to turn off our voice while we are thinking of what to say next. Granted, the constant use of "uh" and "um" can be extremely distracting, and anyone who has this habit should work to control it. Yet, in our opinion, "uh" and "um" are vastly overrated as a speech problem. Speakers have been known to come unglued when they utter a single such sound. An occasional "uh" and "um" in speaking is not nearly as disastrous as some would have us believe. Again, recording your practice session can be a valuable tool in helping you recognize if you have this problem and, if necessary, can help you overcome it.

A technique that has helped some speakers break the "uh" and "um" cycle is to overdo it in practice. Every time you catch yourself saying "uh" or "um" repeat it two or three additional times. Overemphasis on any fault draws it more clearly to your attention. Awareness is the most important step in learning to control this problem. Complete familiarity with your presentation topic, to prevent your being at a loss for words, will also help.

▲ **Voice-quality** problems—a voice that is nasal, thin, harsh, pinched, or breathy—may be difficult to overcome. You can minimize the effect of such problems, though, by working with a speech coach.

▲ **Voice drop** at the end of a sentence is another common fault among speakers. Without realizing it, many people let the last few words trail off to the point where it becomes difficult or impossible to hear them. Consequently, the meaning they are trying to convey is lost or distorted. Since most offenders aren't even aware that they have this problem, it may take a careful review of your taped practice session to help you identify and overcome it.

▲ **Faulty pronunciation** is distracting to the audience and undermines their confidence in the speaker. When your audience has to take time out to identify your words, they are not going to give you their undivided attention. If you are not absolutely certain of the proper way to pronounce a word, look it up in the dictionary. Mispronounced names, too, can be serious gaffes. To be sure you pronounce names correctly, check with someone who knows the pronunciation.

▲ **Poor enunciation** means that you fail to articulate your words satisfactorily. It's like talking with your mouth full. Sometimes poor enunciation can completely change the meaning of a sentence. Consider this. Your message is, "Caring is everything. Nothing matters in this world but caring." However, if you have tendency to pronounce your "ing" endings like "en," it results in "Karen is everythin'. Nothin' matters in this world but Karen." A totally different meaning! Proper enunciation, on the other hand, results in your word projection being clear, precise, and easy to listen to. Consonants (particularly the final ones), and not the vowels, are the real keys to loud and clear communication. Avoid sounding affected.

▲ **Speaking in a monotone voice** can be deadly to your presentation. The message this sends to your audience is one of indifference. If you normally don't have an expressive voice, here are a few techniques you may find helpful.

- Describe the best business deal you ever made or have ever heard of—how it happened, why it happened, what you or someone else did that was right, and how you felt about it.

- Recall the best vacation you ever had in your life. Assume you're a travel agent and are talking to prospective clients about a getaway. You have to convince them that they should go where you went, see what you saw, feel what you felt, and understand why you highly recommend this vacation mecca.

- Another suggestion is to begin reading stories out loud that have a lot of dialogue in them. For example, give each of the characters in a children's story a different voice. This will help you explore your vocal qualities. If you want to test out how you're doing, invite a young child to listen to you. If they're listening with excitement, you're doing great! If they tell you they want to do something else—keep trying.

To correct any faults in how you use your voice, approach the problem systematically. First, become aware of these faults by having co-workers or a speech coach critique your delivery or by reviewing a recorded dry run of your presentation. Study how to correct your voice faults, seeking help from others if necessary. Then, practice incorrectly as well as correctly, to get a feel for how ineffective and effective techniques sound and the difference between them.

Only you can determine how much attention you should pay to your vocal techniques, but remember that almost everyone can improve his or her presentations through careful attention to these basic speech elements and common problems. Remember, good presentations are good conversations.

How Can You Use Common Presentation Tools Effectively?

There are a number of devices that can facilitate the delivery of your message. The two most universally used are the lectern and the pointer.

Lectern or Speaker's Stand

Depending on the type and size, the lectern can serve several purposes, in addition to providing a surface on which to place your notes:

▲ It provides out-of-sight storage space for your visuals and handouts, with convenient access when you need them.

▲ It gives you a place to rest your hands, although you should avoid gripping it tensely.

▲ It serves as a tool for establishing a particular type of relationship with your audience. This is one of the most subtle yet effective uses. Remaining behind the lectern tends to create a more formal relationship, which can be desirable at times. Moving to the side or in front of the lectern, as well as providing a change of pace, tends to remove the physical and an unseen psychological barrier, making for a closer, more informal relationship with audience members. Moving back behind the lectern is a good way to focus attention on your summary, setting it off as a more formal part of your presentation.

Pointer

The pointer can be a valuable tool for drawing attention to specific items on a visual. However, all too frequently it becomes a distracting toy. Beware of using the pointer as a pendulum or a fencing foil, tapping it, or otherwise allowing it to call inappropriate attention to itself. Use the pointer only for its intended purpose, then *put it down when you're through with it!*

This also applies to using a laser pointer. If you are nervous using it, it will be immediately apparent to your audience, as this type of pointer is very sensitive to movement. Practice using a laser pointer until you feel comfortable with it. Also, when you use a laser pointer, make sure you have a backup battery.

How and When Do You Handle Audience Questions?

Most business and governmental presentations provide for an audience-question period. It gives you an excellent opportunity to respond to any uncertainties your audience may have and it involves your audience actively, which helps them mentally review and clarify the message that you have presented. Yet many an otherwise well-delivered presentation may have left a poor impression precisely because of the speaker's inept handling of audience questions.

How you conduct the question period can often have a greater effect on your objectives than the balance of your presentation; therefore, you must carefully plan exactly how and when you will deal with questions. Furthermore, you should anticipate the types of questions and the types of questioners you may face and plan how you will respond to them.

In Chapter 2 we discussed the audience retention curve, the typical variations in the level of your audience's attention *and retention* that you can expect during your presentation. Let's briefly review the topic of audience retention from the standpoint of how it affects your choice of timing for your question period.

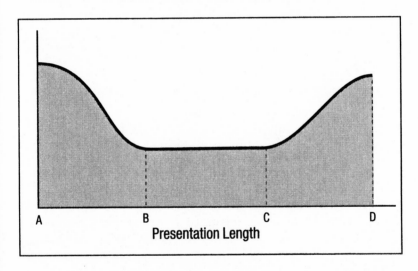

The basic pattern of audience retention is one of heightened attention at the beginning of a presentation, followed by a lower level of attention throughout the main content, and culminating with a rise in both attention and retention at the end. What does this tell us about when to handle audience questions?

Frequently, questions *follow* the presentation, and from the standpoint of accomplishing your presentation objectives, this is often the *poorest* time for them. By turning "prime time" (period D) over to your audience, you run the risk of having them leave your presentation remembering your difficulty in handling an embarrassing question or a "curve" someone may have thrown you. There's also the chance that someone will take up this time asking an interesting question or raising an issue that is totally irrelevant to your presentation.

Handling questions *during* a presentation can be the most effective method. This is when the questions are most meaningful to the people asking them. Furthermore, audience questions provide you with excellent feedback on whether or not your message is being received correctly. And since questions during your presentation require active participation by the audience, they will raise the level of retention during what otherwise might be a down period. But there are problems, too, with taking questions during your presentation. If you are on a tight schedule, lengthy questions may prevent you from completing your presentation on time. Unless the questions are interesting to the entire audience, some listeners may feel their time is being wasted and may lose interest in the balance of your presentation. A premature question may also upset the way you had planned to develop your material. It takes a great deal of skill to handle questions effectively during your presentation and still maintain control and continuity.

There is a compromise approach that you can use in cases where you have been told that the audience question period will come after rather than during your presentation. Consider taking questions *before you present your summary* (period C). Since the final minutes of your presentation are "prime time" for audience retention, you can reserve that for your closing. A simple statement such as, "I'll be happy to answer any questions you may have, but I would like to hold the final two or three minutes for a summary," can give you the control you need. You can then use your summary to recover from any irrelevant, embarrassing, or critical questions and send your audience away with *your* ideas, not someone else's.

As an interest-building technique, consider leaving some important information out of the formal part of your presentation, anticipating a question related to it from someone in your audience. If an audience member does ask about it, your entire audience will get a feeling of participation. At the same time, you will improve your own image by showing how effectively you can answer the question. Also, this will give you some reserve ammunition with which to counteract any opposing points of view that may head your way. If your intentional omission is not questioned by your audience, you can work the material into your summary.

How Do You Conduct an Audience Question Period?

How you handle the question period can be one of the most significant factors in the success or failure of your presentation; accordingly, here are some key pointers to keep mind.

▲ **Your attitude** is definitely the most important single consideration. If you approach questions as if your audience were trying to put you on the spot or catch you in a mistake, you are bound to become defensive. If, on the other hand, you approach questions as if your audience were paying you a compliment by showing their interest in your topic, the difference in your relationship with your audience can be tremendous. In fact, this attitude can be completely disarming to anyone who might be trying to "shoot you down." "I'm so glad you asked that question, Paul. It gives me an opportunity to point out some of the other features of this system."

▲ **Preparedness** is another key to your success. Use your Audience Analysis Audit to review who your listeners will be and to consider the types of questions they might ask. If you anticipate such questions, it gives you an opportunity to plan answers that will reinforce your presentation objectives. You may also want to ask your colleagues to listen to your presentation and ask challenging questions to give you an opportunity to practice answering them.

Another aspect of preparedness is learning to spot, ahead of time, any potentially weak areas in your presentation so that you will not be overly embarrassed if someone challenges them. For example, a government official who was requesting an increased budget to hire eight hundred . additional employees did not help his cause by being unable to satisfactorily explain why the department had not filled the current two hundred vacancies.

Your careful, objective analysis should reveal most such areas of weakness. Try to study recordings of your practice sessions in order to spot places where you might be challenged or get a co-worker to play devil's advocate during your dry run. Then, either develop satisfactory answers for the difficult questions you anticipate or, at the very least, decide what response you will give if someone raises such questions.

This anticipation is particularly beneficial for the nontechnical person presenting information to a technical audience. For example, let's assume you are a marketing representative from XYZ technical company and are presenting information on a new device your company has developed. Although you may not have been part of the development of the device, you are there to present it to that audience in anticipation of a possible purchase. Practicing your presentation in front of the technical people who developed the device, fielding their questions, and answering confidently will add tremendously to your credibility. You may also wish to have a technical person from your company go with you to your presentation. Caution: Make sure that any such people who may accompany you are coached in effective communication skills to avoid having them lose your audience by giving too much detailed information.

▲ **Tact** is an essential ability in fielding audience questions. It often becomes necessary either to clarify exactly what information the questioner desires or to check your understanding of the question. Without embarrassing the individual, you can repeat or paraphrase the question to be sure of its true meaning.

▲ **Phrasing** your responses in terms of their relevance to your presentation objectives is another crucial skill. You may even have to pause for a few seconds to think about a ques-

---

Principles for Handling Questions

▲ Project a positive attitude.

▲ Be prepared for all questions.

▲ Be tactful to all questioners.

▲ Keep the exchange relevant.

▲ Respond to you audience's needs.

---

tion before you attempt to answer it. The ability to make a quick mental evaluation and then provide an answer is one of the hallmarks of an effective presenter. It is a skill that requires constant, disciplined practice. If you control the urge to blurt out an immediate answer and pause to make such an evaluation, you will gain a great advantage.

Often, providing a detailed answer to an irrelevant question will do little to help you accomplish your presentation objectives (even if you happen to be in a position to respond in considerable detail). If such a question is asked, you should comment very briefly only on those factors that have a direct bearing on your objectives. If the questioner is not satisfied with an abbreviated answer, offer to discuss the issue in greater depth after your presentation. "That's an interesting question, Mary, but it seems to be more related to the ABC project. I'll be happy to fill you in on that after the meeting."

▲ If you are **presenting before a large audience** that may not be able to hear the question, always repeat it for the entire audience to hear. If the question is lengthy and you need to paraphrase it, be sure to ask the questioner if you've interpreted it correctly.

▲ And finally, you must project an **air of responsiveness** in handling audience questions. Always give some sort of answer, even if it's "I don't know, but I'll find out and get back to you." Each question must be dealt with somehow or your image will suffer in the collective mind of your audience. Also, when you answer a question, involve your entire audience through your eye contact, not just the person who asked the question.

How Do You Handle Difficult Types of Questions?

There are certain questions that may be difficult to answer or that may divert you from your message if they are not handled properly. Here are some that occur frequently, together with some effective ways of handling them.

▲ If a question touches on a topic that you will cover later in your presentation, say so and give a condensed answer, indicating that you will be providing more detail later. Don't postpone the answer completely, unless it will seriously impair the flow of your material. In fact, repeating the point later will reinforce the idea you had been planning to get across. "Thank you for raising that point, Alice. We are also concerned about that and have developed a contingency plan that I will be covering when we get to delivery schedules. Please ask your question again if it is not clear at that time."

▲ If the question is diversionary, and might lead the discussion away from your objectives, answer it briefly. Then take a moment to summarize where the discussion was prior to the question, in order to bring your audience back on target and ensure the continuity of the presentation. "Yes, I believe Competitor X is developing a similar product but I understand they are at least six months away from releasing it. As I pointed out, our product will be ready in three weeks and will have these unique features . . ."

▲ If you get a buckshot question (several questions in one), you should either zero in on one precise point or ask the questioner to indicate more specifically what he or she is referring to. Narrowing the focus of the question to the point where you can provide a loud and clear response is much better than attempting to answer an entire broad question with vague generalities. "Your question about lead times for customized products is especially valid, Jim. Here's how we plan to handle that . . ."

▲ If you anticipate particularly tough questions, you may wish to ask your audience to write them on cards and send them to the front of the room at the start of the question period. (Be sure cards and pens or pencils are available if you do this.)

There may be some situations where using cards is impractical, and you will need to answer difficult questions as they are asked. You may need a few seconds to think, either because you have to reevaluate the question or because it catches you off guard (that is, you know the answer but need some time to collect your thoughts). *Pause.* These few moments of silence will actually enhance your credibility. Or you can try one of the following:

- "Would you mind repeating the question [or "restating the question in different words"] so that I can be sure I understand you?"

- "Your question definitely gets right to the heart of the issue. What's your position on that?"

- "That's an excellent question. Let's think about it for a few moments." (Pause until you are ready to answer.)

- "That question has certain interesting implications. How do some of the rest of you feel about it?"

- If the question lends itself to such treatment, write it or the answer on a flipchart, a transparency, or a white-board. This can provide you with some thinking time.

▲ If someone asks a question you can't come up with an answer for, *admit it* and refer to someone who *can* answer or offer to find out the answer later. Bluffing is always a bad way out. Not only do you fail to satisfy the questioner, but you also raise doubts in the audience about the truth-fulness of your entire presentation. While most of us are strongly tempted to protect our own egos by muddling through—in hopes that no one will catch our weakness—

it's a temptation you must resist! "Unfortunately, I don't have a ready answer for that one, Arthur. I'll ask Carol to call you this afternoon with that information. She is the engineer who has been working on that feature."

How Do You Handle Difficult Questioners?

Whenever you conduct a question period, you run a risk. You may have some people in your audience with a personal agenda that may not contribute to your presentation objectives. You must develop skills for dealing with people who will use your question time for their own purposes. You should remember, however, that you have two primary responsibilities—first, to do justice to the material you are presenting, and, second, to meet the needs of the entire audience, not just a single member (unless, of course, that single member is a *key individual* who must make the decisions). Here are a few suggestions for dealing with some of the problems that most often arise.

The Argumentative Individual

You must divert the combative type who attempts to get you into a one-on-one debate over a particular topic. In doing so, however, keep this in mind: even if you can prove that you are right, you nearly always lose such an argument. First, the attacker probably won't let go even when proven wrong. Second, an extended argument is usually of little interest to the rest of your audience, and you can lose *them* in the process. Third, if you make the aggressive individual look foolish, the rest of your audience may identify with him or her and resent you for it.

Although there are exceptions, a person who argues in public is primarily seeking recognition, both from you and the rest of your audience. An argument is an opportunity to demonstrate personal knowledge and capability or to air a particular gripe.

What's the best way to deal with an arguer? *If recognition is what is really being sought, give it and get on with your question period.* "You've raised some interesting ideas, Bob. I'd like to take the time to explore them in more detail with you. Can we get together right after the meeting?" You might lose a few points, but the outcome won't be nearly as disastrous as it would be if you were to stop everything and trade verbal punches.

If you do have a satisfactory answer for such a question that won't antagonize your audience, try something like: "Thanks for raising that question, Bob. I appreciate your point of view. We think that _____ will take care of that problem. I'll be glad to meet with you after the session and discuss it in more detail if you wish. Now, as I was saying . . ."

The Curve or Loaded Question

The loaded question is specifically designed to embarrass you or put you on the defensive. Frequently it can't be answered, or it hints that you are trying to hide something. A typical curve might go like this: "How do we know that you can correct these outrageous problems, even if you do get authorization for overtime?"

Like the arguer, this type of questioner is usually seeking recognition. She or he is, in effect, inviting you to "top this." The questioner asks the question knowing full well what your answer will be and generally has a counterquestion ready to zap you with the minute you finish your response. In addition to the techniques recommended for dealing with the arguer, try pulling a turnabout on that individual: "That's a very interesting question, Barbara. How would *you* handle it?" If the game really is one-upmanship, you then have the home-team advantage. But, as with the argumentative individual, prolonging such a discussion offers no benefits. The quicker you can get off the subject, the better.

The Long-Winded Questioner

The rambler digresses all over the place or has to tell you a life history before getting to the point. If you allow this person to drone on indefinitely, you will lose valuable time as well as the interest and attention of the rest of your audience. If possible, you should keep this individual from losing face when you intervene. You can sometimes do this by putting the issue off until after the meeting. Or, try one of these methods:

▲ If you can anticipate the question, jump in at the first opportunity *and* ask and answer the question for the individual. "You would like to know if we can meet the proposed schedule. Let me tell you how we plan to address that."

▲ Pick out a word or an idea that is being expressed and show its relationship to something you or someone else has said previously. "Your point about color is well taken, Warren. Our development team test-marketed this product and green was selected, three to one, over any other color we were considering."

▲ As a last resort *only*, cut the questioner off in the interests of time. Let him or her down easily and give recognition if you can in order to avoid antagonizing the individual or the rest of the audience. Sometimes it helps to "interrupt with a bonus" by offering something extra. "That's very interesting, Connie. I wish we had the time to go into it as thoroughly as we should. I'll be happy to send you a copy of the complete report if that would interest you."

The Takeover Specialist

This dominating type lets you do the work of getting an audience together, then uses the question period to make a speech of his or her own! Whether this unsolicited soliloquy is relevant or not, the loss of control such a situation represents may keep you from achieving your *own* objectives. Luckily, an audience is usually quick to note these tactics. The initial interest generated by this soapbox artist soon wanes, and the audience begins to wonder what *this* has to do with anything. "What is your question, Sam?" or "May we have your question, please?" are polite but assertive responses that demonstrate to your audience not only that you are in control, but that you value their time enough not to waste it.

We could write much more on this most critical and controversial aspect of effective presentations. The important point to remember is that your audience must understand that you welcome questions as a chance to make sure they fully comprehend both the content of your presentation and the actions expected of them.

Valuable Tips for Using Presentation Techniques

Effective presentation techniques add the polish to any well prepared presentation. Keep this in mind as you proceed.

- ▲ **Use two-way communication.** Establish a dialogue, not a monologue, with your audience. Understand the process of delivering a listener-oriented message that increases the probability of getting the response you want.

- ▲ To **overcome fear of speaking,** analyze your audience, conduct an individual audience survey, prepare for likely questions, complete and review the various guidelines and worksheets, visualize your presentation as a success, and prepare yourself physically and mentally.

- ▲ **Skillfully use techniques** related to eye contact, appearance, gestures, body movements, and facial expressions while avoiding distracting mannerisms.

- ▲ Control **speech elements** such as pitch, poor voice quality, intensity, and rate while overcoming any vocal problems (the "uh, um" habit, voice drop, faulty pronunciation, poor enunciation, and speaking in a monotone).

- ▲ Become proficient with **presentation tools** such as a lectern or speaker's stand, and a pointer.

- ▲ Improve your effectiveness in **handling audience questions,** particularly in handling difficult kinds of questions and questioners.

▲ If you choose to take questions at the end of your presentation, make sure you deliver your closing summary *after* the question period.

▲ Remember, good presentations are good conversations that come through *loud and clear.*

5

Handling Presentation Logistics

You've developed the content of your presentation, created or arranged for your visuals and other support materials, and carefully designed your delivery approach. One final hurdle remains before you can actually deliver your presentation. You must give proper attention to your presentation logistics—the nitty-gritty details of room setup, audience notification, lighting, name tags, and a host of other such considerations.

"Wait just a minute," you may reply. "It's my job to give the presentation, not play janitor or meeting coordinator. I've got enough to worry about. Let somebody *else* take care of those details." This sounds like a reasonable attitude—until you stop to consider that *your* presentation will suffer if these details are not handled properly.

If the room setup hampers your audience's view; if a piece of equipment isn't delivered to the meeting site; or if individuals whose presence is vital fail to attend (either because the original notification was not sufficiently persuasive or because there was insufficient follow-up), *you* will be the one with egg on your face. If the "somebody else" who is responsible for logistics fails to follow through effectively, it's *your* presentation (and its objectives) that may go down in flames.

We admit that managing logistics involves extra work, but this work is vital to accomplishing your objectives. Just as you, the presenter, need to be involved in planning the content of your presentation and in developing your accompanying visuals and support materials, so it is with handling your meeting arrangements.

Does this mean that you must personally attend to all the minutiae? Hardly! It *does* mean that you must provide personal input and guidance to make certain that the right questions are being asked and the right issues are being addressed. It means that you must closely supervise or follow up with all the "somebody elses" who are assigned to take care of the logistical details. It means—in short—that *you* must assume overall responsibility for managing your *entire* presentation.

The balance of this chapter will address the principal types of presentation logistics you must deal with. The main concerns are:

▲ Inviting audience members to attend your presentation.

▲ Arranging the room setup.

▲ Preparing the specifications for audiovisual equipment and for your visuals and other support materials.

▲ Handling the special logistical challenges that arise in making an off-site presentation.

In addition, there are a number of fine points that are so nearly self-explanatory that they require little more than listing here, but that could nonetheless prove embarrassing or even disastrous if they were overlooked.

At the end of this chapter you will find a Presentation Logistics Checklist, a tool that can help you handle the logistics of your meeting in an organized fashion and with minimal expenditure of your time and effort. This gives both you and those who will be assisting you a clear record of **who** will be doing **what**. This checklist covers the basic issues that should receive attention prior to most presentations. You may wish to add other items that need to be checked beforehand in connection with a particular presentation you will be making.

Has Your Audience Been Satisfactorily Notified?

If you address the following questions in advance, you will increase the probability of having the appropriate people attend your presentation.

▲ Have all the right people—those most directly concerned or those who can make the necessary decisions—been invited to attend your presentation?

▲ How were they notified—by letter, memo, phone call, e-mail, formal announcement, word of mouth?

▲ Did the notification give enough (and correct) information about the topic of your presentation, its purpose, time and location, and so forth?

▲ How persuasive was the notification?

▲ Do you know who has agreed to attend?

▲ Has there been a follow-up with those who were invited but have not yet replied?

For the best results, you should either prepare the notice yourself or provide detailed guidance to the person who will handle notifications. Never lose sight of the fact that attendance by the right people is vital to accomplishing your presentation objectives. Give them a reason to come.

How Is the Room Set Up?

Your choice of the many possible room setup options will depend on the size and shape of the meeting room, the size and nature of your audience, the type of presentation and delivery method, and the kind of participation you want from your audience members.

This section discusses some of the more conventional seating arrangements and their applications. The recommended square footage allowed for each participant is based on a rectangular room without visual obstructions. Allow additional space if the presentation room has an unusual shape, columns, or other peculiarities that might interfere with your audience's vision. When you calculate total room capacity that you will need, be sure to allow from 40 to 100 additional square feet for yourself and any presentation accessories you plan to use.

Among your general considerations, regardless of the particular setup you use, will be:

▲ Making certain there are enough tables and chairs for the anticipated number of attendees.

▲ Deciding whether separate seating is required for special guests.

▲ Determining whether you will need a lectern, a table for your aids and supplies, a microphone, or a platform from which to speak.

Auditorium Style (8 square feet per person)

 This arrangement is useful for large groups in which there is little or no need for the audience to write or consult reference materials. With this arrangement, audience participation is usually limited to questions and discussion.

Classroom Style (16 square feet per person)

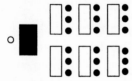 This arrangement is useful for relatively formal situations in which participants will need to write or actively use reference materials. Again, with this arrangement, audience participation is usually limited to questions and discussion.

Conference Style (20 square feet per person)

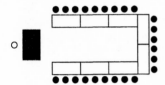 This arrangement is useful for small groups (usually ten people or fewer) in which extensive discussion is desirable, in which your audience members will be writing a considerable amount, and in which they will be actively using reference materials.

Horseshoe or U-shape Style (20 square feet per person)

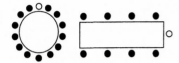 This arrangement is useful where eye contact with individual audience members, writing or using materials by participants, and open, relatively informal discussion are all desirable.

Buzz Style (20 to 24 square feet per person)

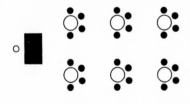 This arrangement is useful when you will conduct small group discussion as part of your presentation. Round tables for each group are preferred.

Herringbone Style (20 square feet per person)

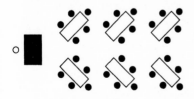 This arrangement is also useful for group discussions. It is more formal than the buzz style and less formal than the classroom style. Rectangular tables are used.

You could, of course, come up with many variations on these basic arrangements. The key to your success in this area—whether you choose one of the standard arrangements shown or devise an arrangement of your own—is to use a setup that will best support the achievement of your presentation objectives.

What About Your Equipment?

The choice and availability of equipment can **make or break** your presentation. Consider the following questions carefully and be certain that you know the answers.

▲ Is the equipment required for your presentation visuals and other support materials located in the room where your presentation will take place?

▲ Do you need a projection table or a place to display your materials?

▲ Is the projection equipment set up so the audience will have an unobstructed view of your visuals?

▲ Where are the electrical outlets? Phone outlets? Will you need an extension cord?

▲ Do the outlets accept the type of power plug on your equipment, or do you need an adapter?

▲ Do you need a surge protector for your electronic equipment?

▲ Is it safe to operate your equipment using an adapter or extension cord?

▲ Is your equipment working properly? Do you have a spare projection bulb?

▲ If you are using a computer, is your presentation software program loaded and operating correctly?

▲ Are the proper cables attached to project the computer images?

▲ Is your projector focused?

▲ Have you checked the room to determine whether—and how—you can control the lighting? Do the windows have shades, blinds, or curtains to eliminate glare? Have you figured out how to operate the curtains or blinds if the room must be darkened?

▲ Have you arranged for a flipchart or whiteboard, if needed?

▲ Do you have marking pens (and in the colors you will require)? Have you checked to make sure the pens haven't dried out?

▲ Do you have the proper marking pens if you plan to use a whiteboard? Do you have an eraser?

▲ Do you have masking tape or self-adhering sheets for posting flipchart pages on the walls?

▲ Are your transparencies, slides, or other visuals arranged in the proper order?

▲ Is a pointer available? If you are using a laser pointer, does it work? Do you have spare batteries?

▲ If you have handouts for distribution, has an adequate number been reproduced? Are they assembled in the correct order and stored out of sight of your audience? Have you made provisions to distribute them at the proper time and not before?

▲ If you are using workbooks, have they been placed where you want them?

▲ Do your audience members have pens or pencils for taking notes?

▲ If you plan to display objects or models, are they stored in the desired order and out of sight of your audience? If this is not possible, have you arranged for a suitable cover to shield these items from your audience's view until they are needed?

▲ Have you made provisions or set aside time after your presentation for audience members to examine objects or models more carefully?

What About Off-Site Presentations?

Precisely because the presentation will be off-site (not at your own location), you need to work with and rely on someone from that particular site. Find out:

▲ Who is the primary person to contact about coordinating arrangements at the presentation site?

▲ Has a detailed specification sheet and/or room diagram been provided to this coordinator?

▲ Have arrangements been made to procure, ship, carry, or rent all of the necessary audiovisual/computer equipment you will need?

▲ If these items will arrive ahead of time, can they be stored safely and securely until you get there?

▲ Will an on-site audiovisual equipment coordinator be available to assist with setup or help overcome problems?

▲ Will your travel schedule permit you to arrive early enough to make last-minute adjustments to the meeting arrangements, if necessary?

▲ Will you have prior access to the room in which your presentation will be conducted?

▲ If you do not plan to take all of your equipment or support materials home with you after the presentation, have you arranged for them to be shipped back to your office and for them to be stored in a secure location until they are shipped?

What Are Some Other Key Issues to Address?

The following list provides a brief reminder about a number of additional logistical matters that may require your attention:

▲ **Reservations.** Is the planned meeting site available to you on an ongoing basis, or must you reserve it? If a reservation is required, has someone been assigned the responsibility for making it?

▲ **Seating.** We talked earlier about room setup—how the tables, chairs, and lectern will be placed. Within that overall arrangement, you need to be sensitive to issues of seating "protocol." Is it OK for anyone to sit anywhere, or must all seats or certain seats be reserved or assigned?

▲ **Distractions.** Have you identified potential visible or audible distractions that you should compensate for?

- Can you arrange for audience members to receive telephone messages during breaks or after your session rather than interrupt your presentation?

- Will you ask audience members to turn off beepers and cellular phones during your presentation?

- If there is a telephone in the meeting room, have you arranged for it to be removed or shut off during your presentation?

- If that is not possible, have you arranged for someone not directly involved with your presentation to answer the phone and take messages?

▲ **Ventilation and smoking.** Is ventilation adequate to keep the room comfortable?

- Do you know where the heating and air conditioning controls are located and how to operate them?

- Do you need to have a staff member make temperature adjustments?

- How do you contact that person?

Many sites do not allow smoking.

- Is there a smoking area?

- Have smokers been informed of its location?

▲ **Registration.** Do participants need to register? If so, how will this be handled?

▲ **Identification.** Will each audience member need to have a name tent in front of his or her seat?

- Will audience members wear name tags?

- Will you put people's names on these in advance (being sure to double-check spelling)?

- Will you provide markers and blank cards or tags and have audience members letter their own?

  You can put out preprinted name tents in front of where you want each audience member to sit as a simple means of controlling the seating arrangement.

▲ **Food, beverages, breaks.**

- Has the location of rest rooms been clearly identified for participants?
- Will there be planned breaks?
- Would it be desirable to provide coffee, soft drinks, or water either during the session or during a break?
- Will there be a meal break?
- How much break time should be allotted?

These issues are neither time-consuming nor complex to deal with. If you address them prior to your presentation, you can make the mechanics of your session proceed much more smoothly and ensure that your message comes through *loud and clear.*

Presentation Logistics Worksheet

Presentation topic:_____

Presenter(s): _____

Meeting coordinator: _____

Date:_____ Time:_____

Address or building: _____ Room No.: _____

Site contact person:_____ Phone: _____

1. Attendance

    No. of audience members notified: _____

    No. of positive replies received: _____

    Expected total attendance: _____

2. Room Setup

Rank in order of your preference:

☐ Auditorium   ☐ Conference   ☐ Buzz

☐ Classroom   ☐ Horseshoe   ☐ Herringbone

☐ Other (specify):_____

Sketch the setup you want in the space provided, using the standard symbolism indicated on the left. Clearly show such relevant details as the layout of tables and chairs and the number of persons per table.

Tables

● Chair

○ Presenter

▮ Lectern

╱ Screen

Presentation Logistics Worksheet Checklist, Continued

3. Room Considerations

	Status*	Responsibility	Comments
Chairs			
Tables			
Seating protocol			
Lectern			
Platform			
Microphone			
Lighting			
Windows			
Distractions			
Telephone/messages			
Ventilation			
Smoking/ashtrays			
Temperature control			
Emergency exits			
Name tents or name tags			
Pencils/notepaper			
Registration			
Beverages			
Rest rooms			

* OK = satisfactory   o = not needed   + = requires attention

Presentation Logistics Worksheet Checklist, Continued

4. Presentation Support Materials and Equipment

	Status*	Responsibility	Comments
Needed equipment (list)			
Location of electrical outlets			
Extension cord			
Projection table			
Spare bulbs			
Supplies (masking tape, marking pens, etc.) (list)			
Handouts (list)			

* OK = satisfactory   o = not needed   + = requires attention

CHAPTER
6

In Closing

To plan your business or technical presentation—an *effective* one, that is—you must work backward from your desired results. What are you trying to accomplish? And, is a presentation the best way to accomplish these results?

▲ Broadly speaking, there are **four types of presentations:**

1. **Persuasive,** which is designed to bring your audience around to your point of view on a particular topic.

2. **Explanatory,** which familiarizes your audience with a new topic, usually in general terms.

3. **Instructional,** which actively teaches something to your audience, usually in detail.

4. **Briefing,** which updates your audience on a matter they are already familiar with.

Whatever the specific results are that you seek from your presentation, a systematic, organized approach to preparing and delivering your material, such as the one illustrated in Chapter 1 and repeated here, is the best way to proceed. Use resource materials you selected with your intended audience in mind and design the content that is meaningful to that audience. To put that content across, you create visuals and other support materials that will enhance your message, you use your presentation skills, and you oversee logistical details that affect how smoothly your session will go. Throughout the preparation, achieving productive results is the name of the game—getting your message across in such a way that your audience takes whatever action you intend.

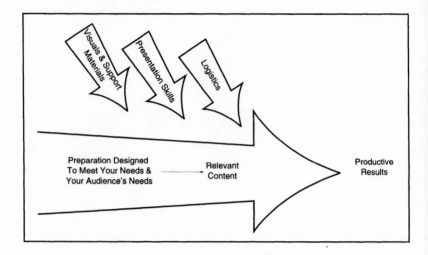

▲ The **preparation process** encompasses the following six steps:

1. **Establish objectives** for your presentation. Determine *why* you are giving the presentation; that is, *what you hope to accomplish* with it. Decide whether your objectives are realistic—in terms of their scope; in terms of your audience's knowledge, background, and ability to take action; and in terms of what you can reasonably expect to achieve. Also give thought to any secondary objectives you might have (ancillary expectations, such as establishing personal credibility), that you may not wish to state openly.

2. **Analyze your audience** in terms of their knowledge, attitudes, and ability to act. Tailor your approach accordingly so that your presentation will most likely accomplish your objectives *with this particular audience.*

3. **Prepare a Preliminary Plan** for your presentation. The Preliminary Plan is a conceptual framework, not a speaking outline. List the objectives you have established for your presentation, summarize the most pertinent information you have gathered about your audience, list the main ideas or concepts your audience must compre-

hend if you are to meet your objectives, and indicate the factual information you need to support and effectively communicate those ideas. Keep your preparation effort focused on results.

4. **Select resource material** for your presentation. Ask yourself a series of open questions based on your Preliminary Plan. When you think you've identified all the resource material on which to base your presentation, submit each item to the "Why?" test to make *sure* it contributes significantly to achieving your objectives.

5. **Organize your material** for effective delivery. Here is where you will prepare your presentation outline. Recognize that your audience will be more attentive at the start of your presentation, considerably less so throughout the midportion, and more attentive again at the end. You should emphasize the two high points in audience attention *and retention* by preparing an *opening* that is brief and interesting and a *closing* that summarizes your purpose and principal points in an arresting manner and that makes an effective appeal for audience action. To maximize audience involvement and attention during the *main content* of your presentation (usually the low point in terms of retention), you should aim to develop and illustrate your main ideas in a lively and varied fashion.

6. **Practice** your presentation in advance and **evaluate** it for necessary modifications. Systematically working the bugs out of your material is essential to preparing any presentation. Practice can involve delivering your presentation aloud by yourself; video- or audiotaping your practice session, to be critiqued by you and by others; or staging a full-scale dry run to be critiqued by you and by knowledgeable members of your practice audience. Focus on assessing your performance to identify areas where you need to improve.

Beyond practicing for just those presentations you are required to make, we strongly recommend that you seek out additional opportunities to practice speaking in front of others. Join Toastmasters. Take a public-speaking course. Volunteer for speaking assignments even if the thought paralyzes you. Experience is the only way to overcome those butterflies, or at least reduce their size. Even the most experienced presenters suffer some anxiety when their moment of truth is at hand, but it is their experience that keeps them from letting their anxiety get in the way of their objectives. If you plan to become a professional speaker at some point or want to know more about the business of speaking for income, contact the National Speakers Association.

▲ **Presentation visuals** and other support materials heighten your audience's retention rate by providing visual support for your message.

- **Illustrating.** To determine which points to illustrate, focus on the main ideas you identified in your Preliminary Plan (the ideas that your audience *must* retain if your presentation is to achieve its objectives).

- **Storyboarding** is a helpful way to systematically match these key ideas with visual concepts.

- **Gathering Visuals.** You can purchase, find, and create visuals. You need to be constantly alert for sources of visuals and other support materials relevant to your customary topics. We recommend that you maintain an art file of raw materials and ideas for visuals and other types of support materials. With such a file as a ready resource, you never have to start from scratch when it comes to preparing your visuals.

- **Communicating.** Never forget that your visuals are a means of helping you communicate your message; they are not a substitute for that message.

- **Practicing.** Practice is vital. When you practice, much of your attention may be devoted to handling your visuals.

With sufficient rehearsal, you will be able to concentrate on delivering your message rather than worrying about your visuals. Your audience will also be able to turn their full attention to the substance of your presentation.

▲ The actual **delivery of your presentation**—the moment all your preparatory work has been leading up to—is based on the premise that your presentation must be listener-oriented. That is, you must aim for the approach that would be most appealing, persuasive, and interesting—not from *your* personal standpoint but from the standpoint of *this specific audience.* The more successful you are, the greater the likelihood that your audience will take the action you desire.

Presentation delivery involves a number of different skill areas, including presentation techniques, vocal techniques, and handling audience questions.

- **Presentation techniques** include such things as eye contact, appearance, gestures, body movements, facial expressions, and avoiding distracting mannerisms.

- **Vocal techniques** address such factors in oral communication as pitch, voice quality, intensity, and rate, as well as avoiding such common speech problems as overuse of "uh," voice drop, faulty pronunciation, poor enunciation, and speaking in a monotone.

- **Handling questions** from your audience is another aspect of delivery that requires considerable thought and advance planning, since the impression you create during the question period often can make or break your presentation.

  ▲ To successfully field your audience's questions, you must start with a positive attitude about being questioned, be thoroughly prepared for whatever questions you can anticipate beforehand, handle questions tactfully, phrase your answers so they are directly relevant to your presentation objectives, and be responsive (to the extent possible) to all audience questions.

▲ You have to hone your skills in responding to those individuals who try to start an argument with you, who toss loaded questions your way, who attempt to take over the floor, or who engage in extensive rambling in the course of asking a question.

▲ Another aspect of planning for a presentation is **handling logistics**. This involves such things as:

• How, when, and by whom will your audience be notified?

• Arranging for a room setup that will meet your needs.

• Taking care of the myriad details associated with using support materials and equipment.

• Handling the logistics peculiar to staging an off-site presentation.

Must you do everything exactly the way this book says in order to make successful presentations? Of course not! What you must do is *communicate effectively;* that is, get your message across in a way that will accomplish your presentation objectives.

Most presenters find that the methods described in this book constitute a highly practical approach to achieving effective communication with a minimum of time, effort, and stress. In short, these methods provide a solid foundation in the art of making business and technical presentations. As you gain experience in making presentations, you can introduce helpful modifications to the techniques advocated here and identify certain cases where it would be advisable to bend the rules we've proposed.

To this we say—If it works, go with it! If members of your audience do what you want them to do as a result of your presentation, you have achieved effective communication—even if you have violated every principle covered in this text!

Here's to shorter, better organized presentations that come across LOUD AND CLEAR!

A

Worksheets and Guidelines

This section of *Loud and Clear* reproduces the most useful worksheets and guidelines from the preceding chapters. We hope that you'll use the worksheets to prepare for your future presentations, and look back at the guidelines to remind yourself of the crucial ingredients of successful presentation-planning.

To use these worksheets most easily, photocopy the pages you want at 129% enlargement onto standard business-size pages. You may use these photocopies yourself, pass them out to colleagues, or reproduce them in other ways for training, as long as the copyright and permission notice remains on each page.

Guidelines for Preparing a Preliminary Plan

Use the Preliminary Plan as a guide:

▲ For you, as the presenter, in selecting your materials, keeping your ideas focused, and determining key emphasis points.

▲ For support personnel who may provide you with backup data, prepare visuals, or assist in the presentation itself.

1. **Identify your specific objectives for this presentation**, keeping in mind one or more of the following criteria:

   • They should answer the question, "Why am I making this presentation?"

   • They should state the results you want from the presentation—in effect, completing the sentence, "I want the following things to happen as a result of this presentation: . . ."

   • If you need to identify the specific project in your objectives, use a sentence such as, "I want to tell about . . . so that . . . will take place."

   • Your objectives should take into consideration any secondary objectives that you want to accomplish with your presentation.

Guidelines for Preparing a Preliminary Plan

2. **Identify the specific audience** for whom you are designing this presentation. State in one or two sentences the pertinent information about the audience's expectations, knowledge, attitudes, and so forth.

3. **State the main ideas or concepts** that your audience *must* comprehend if you are to meet your presentation objectives. These should:

   - Be in conclusion form and, preferably, in complete sentences.
   - Definitely lead to the accomplishment of your specific objectives.
   - Be interesting in themselves or capable of being made so.
   - Be few in number, usually no more than five.

4. **Identify necessary factual information** to support each of your main ideas and make them comprehensible to your audience. Avoid excessive detail.

Preliminary Plan Worksheet

Topic of the presentation: _____

Approximate date, time, and place for the presentation: _____
_____

Who asked for the presentation? _____

Presentation objectives (what will be the immediate results if this presentation is successful?):

1. _____
_____

2. _____
_____

3. _____
_____

4. _____
_____

Audience analysis (who are they, and what is their general knowledge of, interest in, and attitude toward the subject?):

_____
_____
_____
_____
_____
_____
_____
_____
_____
_____

Main ideas or concepts that the audience must comprehend and retain if you are to meet your presentation objectives:

1. _____
   _____
   _____
   _____
   _____

2. _____
   _____
   _____
   _____
   _____

3. _____
   _____
   _____
   _____
   _____

4. _____
   _____
   _____
   _____
   _____

5. _____
   _____
   _____
   _____
   _____

Factual Information necessary to support the main ideas:

Main Idea 1 _____

_____

_____

_____

_____

Main Idea 2 _____

_____

_____

_____

_____

Main Idea 3 _____

_____

_____

_____

_____

Main Idea 4 _____

_____

_____

_____

_____

Main Idea 5 _____

_____

_____

_____

_____

Resource Material Worksheet

Complete the following questionnaire to select what and how much material should be included to effectively support your main ideas. This will ensure that you don't use too much or too little resource material. (Refer to page 42 for complete explanations.)

1. What is the object or purpose of this presentation?

_____

_____

2. What should you cover? What can you eliminate?

_____

_____

3. What amount of detail do you need?

_____

_____

4. What must you say if you are to reach your presentation objectives?

_____

_____

5. What is the best way to say it?

_____

_____

6. What kind of audience action or response are you seeking in order to meet your objectives?

_____

_____

7. What material should you withhold from your presentation but have available for reference if required?

_____

_____

Resource Material Worksheet, Continued

8. Submit all your resource material to the "Why?" test.

_____

_____

Now make a list of all the resource material you will need to include in your presentation. Also make a list of additional material that you should have available for reference, if necessary.

_____

_____

_____

_____

_____

_____

_____

_____

_____

_____

_____

_____

_____

_____

_____

_____

_____

_____

_____

Guidelines for Organizing Your Material

Opening

Your opening has three powerful purposes:

1. Selling your audience on listening to your presentation.
2. Introducing your subject matter.
3. Establishing your personal credibility.

Suggested approaches for your opening include:

▲ **Direct statement** of your subject and why it is important to your audience.

▲ **Indirect opening** dealing with some vital interest of your audience that you can link to your subject.

▲ **Vivid example** or comparison leading directly to your subject.

▲ **Strong quotation** related to your subject.

▲ **Important statistics** related to your subject.

▲ **Story or anecdote** illustrating your subject.

Main Content

In order to confirm that your audience has a clear understanding of the information presented in the body of your presentation, remember:

▲ The appropriate sequence of your main ideas.

▲ Factual information that will support your main ideas.

(Continues next page.)

Guidelines for Organizing Your Material

▲ Ten suggested ways to make your presentation more interesting:

1. Analogies
2. Humor
3. Quotes
4. Personal stories
5. Examples and illustrations
6. Reiteration
7. Statistics
8. Charts and graphs
9. Expert testimony
10. Audience involvement

Closing

Your closing should be a mini-presentation in and of itself. It should paraphrase your opening statements to demonstrate cohesiveness. An effective closing should include one or more of the following:

▲ **Challenge** to your audience.

▲ **Summary** of your main ideas.

▲ Suggested **agreement or recommendation** for action.

▲ Powerful **quote or statistic** that directly relates to your topic.

▲ **Story or anecdote** that drives home the message you want your audience to carry away.

Presentation Worksheet

Presentation topic:_____

Presenter(s): _____

Date, time, place:_____

General Considerations

1. How will the room be arranged (seating, name cards, and so on)?

_____

_____

_____

2. How many people do you expect to attend? How and when will they be notified of the presentation?

_____

_____

_____

3. What presentation aids will be required? Will equipment be available at the presentation site or must someone transport it there?

_____

_____

_____

4. Will you use handouts? What arrangements do you have to make for them? How and when will they be distributed?

_____

_____

_____

5. How and when will you handle audience questions?

_____

_____

_____

Presentation Outline

Time allotted	Content*	Methods, aids, examples

* *Opening:* Sell your audience on listening, introduce the subject, establish personal credibility.
Main Content: Develop your main ideas.
Closing: Summarize content, appeal for action.

Guidelines for Selecting and Designing Presentation Visuals

Key Concepts

An Effective Presentation Visual Must . . .

Visual Representations

▲ Present an idea better than words alone.

> The new model is far easier to use because of the following features: bigger buttons, wheels and battery power.

▲ Represent one key concept (even though it may present a lot of information about the concept).

Easier To Use

Bigger Buttons

Battery Power

Wheels

▲ Emphasize pictures or graphics rather than words, wherever possible.

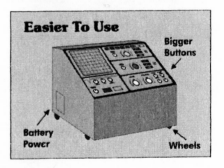

Easier To Use

Bigger Buttons

(Continues next page.)

Key Concepts

Visual Representations

▲ *Generally restrict the use of text to a maximum of four words per line and six lines per visual, emphasizing short phrases or key words rather than complete sentences.*

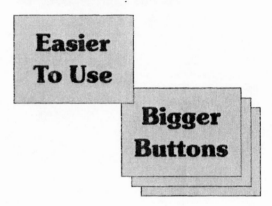

▲ *Use appropriate color, font, and font size.*

Key Concepts

Visual Representations

▲ *Be carefully made: neat, clear, uncluttered.*

Reproduced with permission from *Loud and Clear* by George L. Morrisey, Thomas L. Sechrest, and Wendy B. Warman. Copyright © 1997 by Addison Wesley Longman, Inc.

Guidelines for Using Presentation Media

Visibility

▲ Can your presentation visuals be seen (and heard?) satisfactorily by everyone?

▲ Have you taken into consideration the size of the room, the number of people, proximity to a source of distracting noise, the seating arrangement, visual obstacles, lighting, and so forth?

▲ Have you brought overhead transparencies to use in a huge auditorium with hundreds in your audience? (A projected slide is probably the easiest and least-expensive alternative in this circumstance, though a computer-based presentation can also be projected with specialized equipment.)

▲ Have you followed the development guidelines discussed earlier and used an appropriate type size and properly contrasting colors?

▲ Is there so much information included on your visual that it just doesn't make sense for people who are not sitting close to the source?

Availability and Compatibility

▲ Will the equipment you need to use for displaying presentation visuals be available to you at the presentation site?

▲ Can it be made available at a cost (in terms of money, time, or convenience) that will not exceed its relative value to your presentation?

Guidelines for Using Presentation Media

▲ Can you store the equipment out of sight of your audience before and after use to minimize distraction? A model of a particular piece of machinery, for example, can be effectively used, but it may distract the audience if it is left in view throughout the presentation.

▲ If you are using electronic equipment or a presentation software package, are they compatible? For example, if you are using an LCD (liquid crystal display) panel to project presentation visuals from a laptop computer, is the cable that connects the computer to the panel the correct one?

▲ Does your version of the software package that you used to develop your presentation, which you saved on a disk for portability, match the version available at the presentation site?

▲ Does the computer available at the presentation site support the software that you are using for your presentation?

There are so many options you need to consider when you display your visuals and other support materials that it is easy to become overwhelmed. Don't get carried away! Use common sense to determine the most effective way for you to present your message to *this audience* so it will come across *loud and clear.*

Guidelines for the Effective Use of Visuals and Support Materials

▲ Never use visuals or support materials in front of an audience until you have rehearsed with them.

- Be sure you know how to set up the required equipment properly (or have specialists who can do this for you) and that you know how to use it.

- Practice using your materials. Videotape your practice sessions and critique the videotape, or ask colleagues to provide feedback on your practice session.

▲ Make certain your visuals and support materials are a help rather than a hindrance to your communication.

- Design materials that are simple, clear, and represent facts accurately.

- Demonstrate only one key concept or idea per visual and be sure that the visual conveys the idea or concept better than words alone could.

- Keep the text to a minimum, emphasizing pictures and graphics instead.

- Use appropriate fonts, sizes, colors, contrasts, or other techniques to emphasize or clarify your main points.

▲ Don't waste your audience's time or cause audience distraction with your materials.

- Be sure all necessary equipment, components, and materials are available at the start of your presentation.

- Arrange the components of your presentation in the proper sequence prior to your session.

- Set up and adjust the equipment (or have it done for you) before your audience arrives; ensure that visuals and other support materials can be seen and heard from all locations at the presentation site.

Guidelines for the Effective Use of Visuals and Support Materials, Continued

- Wait until after you complete your presentation and your audience leaves before you pack up your presentation materials.

▲ Project! Speak with more volume than you normally require.

- Remember that your audience's attention is divided between you and the materials you are using to support your spoken words.
- Remember, too, that when you speak in a darkened room, you need more volume to hold your audience's attention.

▲ Don't stand between your audience and a projected image.

- Check to make sure that you aren't part of the projected image!
- Use a pointer to call attention to specific elements of a visual.

▲ Don't let your visuals or support materials distract *you*.

- Face and talk to your audience, not the projected visual.
- Don't interrupt your speaking pace when you change visuals.
- Use visuals and support materials to *support* your message. Avoid modifying your message so that you can use some "neat" technique.

▲ Don't let your visuals or support materials distract your *audience*.

- Don't project a visual until you are ready for it to be seen.
- Use visuals or support materials only when you make direct reference to them.
- When you finish using the materials, turn off the projector or cover up any models. Make sure your audience is paying attention to you and your message.
- Avoid passing items around during your presentation. Either show the objects to the group as a whole or display them after the session.

Presentation Logistics Worksheet

Presentation topic:_____

Presenter(s): _____

Meeting coordinator: _____

Date: _____   Time:_____

Address or building: _____   Room No.: _____

Site contact person:_____   Phone: _____

1. Attendance

No. of audience members notified: _____

No. of positive replies received: _____

Expected total attendance: _____

2. Room Setup

Rank in order of your preference:

☐ Auditorium   ☐ Conference   ☐ Buzz

☐ Classroom   ☐ Horseshoe   ☐ Herringbone

☐ Other (specify):_____

Sketch the setup you want in the space provided, using the standard symbolism indicated on the left. Clearly show such relevant details as the layout of tables and chairs and the number of persons per table.

Tables

● Chair

○ Presenter

■ Lectern

╱ Screen

Presentation Logistics Worksheet Checklist, Continued

3. Room Considerations

	Status*	Responsibility	Comments
Chairs			
Tables			
Seating protocol			
Lectern			
Platform			
Microphone			
Lighting			
Windows			
Distractions			
Telephone/messages			
Ventilation			
Smoking/ashtrays			
Temperature control			
Emergency exits			
Name tents or name tags			
Pencils/notepaper			
Registration			
Beverages			
Rest rooms			

* OK = satisfactory   o = not needed   + = requires attention

Presentation Logistics Worksheet Checklist, Continued

4. Presentation Support Materials and Equipment

	Status*	Responsibility	Comments
Needed equipment (list)			.
			.
Location of electrical outlets			
Extension cord			.
Projection table			.
Spare bulbs			
Supplies (masking tape, marking pens, etc.) (list)			
Handouts (list)			

* OK = satisfactory   o = not needed   + = requires attention

APPENDIX

B

Annotated Resources

There are thousands of books, software packages, audiotapes, videotapes, films, training courses, and other products on the market related to preparing and delivering presentations. We won't attempt to list them all here. We encourage you to browse on the World Wide Web, in bookstores, libraries, management journals, and other professional publications for further information and guidance. However, we have described a few resources here that are of general interest and that we have found especially useful.

BOOKS

Antion, Thomas S. *Wake 'em Up: How to Use Humor and Other Professional Techniques to Create Alarmingly Good Business Presentations.* Landover Hills, Md.: Anchor, 1997. This is a content-rich publication on making effective presentations ranging from international speaking to sales presentations to the how-tos of getting licensing for copyrighted music you want to use in your presentations. We particularly like the information on humor, including Humor Placement, Humor Risk, Humorous Acknowledgments to Tough Situations, 34 Ways to Be Funny, I Like Humor: Where Can I Find It?, and five tips to being funny while using audiovisuals.

Ball, Patricia Ann. *Straight Talk Is More Than Words.* Granville, Ohio: Knox Publishing, 1996. Patricia Ball is a professional speaker and actor who knows how to make the best use of your total communication presence. This book capitalizes on ·

her theatrical training and experience, showing you how to really connect with your audience. Her chapters "As You Speak" and "Mechanics of Speech Delivery," in particular, provide excellent insights as well as useful techniques for coming across as an effective presenter.

Bedrosian, Maggie. *Speak Like a Pro: A Business Tool for Marketing and Managing*. Rockville, Md.: BCI Press, 1994. If you want a fresh, focused, and functional guide for improving your impact in speeches, at meetings, and on television, this book is power-packed with great ideas you can use. Particularly helpful are the "Emergency 10-Minutes-to-Prepare Panic Plan" and the "Speaking Skill Development Inventory."

Booher, Dianna. *67 Presentation Secrets to Wow Any Audience: Your Guide to Clear, Concise, Persuasive Presentations*. Minneapolis, Minn.: Lakewood Books, 1995. This book is a problem-solving gold mine for speakers. We especially like the sections on "Developing a Natural Delivery Style" and "Handling Question-and-Answer Periods."

————. *Communicate with Confidence! How to Say It Right the First Time and Every Time*. New York: McGraw-Hill, 1994. In this book, Dianna Booher provides us with more than 1,000 specific tips on communicating effectively with others. Of particular value to people making technical presentations is the section on "Winning People Over to Your Way of Thinking: Being Persuasive."

Brandt, Richard C. *Flip Charts: How to Draw Them and How to Use Them*. San Diego: University Associates, 1986. This is a fun and practical paperback that describes for experts and beginning presenters alike the skills needed to use flip charts effectively.

Decker, Bert, with James Denney. *You've Got to Be Believed to Be Heard*. New York: St. Martin's Press, 1993. This groundbreaking approach to personal communications examines how to persuade by winning emotional trust. It contains practical exercises to improve voice, posture, expressiveness, gestures, eye contact, and more.

Detz, Joan. *Can You Say a Few Words?* New York: St. Martin's Press, 1991. Have you ever heard that question asked at a meeting or other occasion? Here's what you can do to be a successful presenter in such a situation.

Frank, Milo. *How to Get Your Point Across in 30 Seconds—or Less.* New York: Simon & Schuster, 1986. One of the classics in the field, this little book is a veritable gold mine of concepts and techniques for hooking your audience and keeping them tuned in to your message.

Gilbert, Frederick, Ph.D. *PowerSpeaking®: How Ordinary People Can Make Extraordinary Presentations.* Redwood City, Calif.: Frederick Gilbert Associates, 1996. Rick Gilbert's driving philosophy about the art and practice of public speaking is "It's not about perfection." He and his organization help speakers who care deeply about what they're saying make their delivery live up to their passion. A particularly valuable section of his book focuses on developing and using stories that persuade.

Glickstein, Lee. *Be Heard Now! How to Compel Rapt Attention Every Time You Speak.* San Francisco: Leeway Press, 1996. Lee Glickstein developed the Transformational Speaking® approach to help him overcome his stage fright. This is a gem of a book for those who want to overcome their fear and be genuinely authentic with their audiences. Glickstein's technique guides speakers to structure their talks in a way that reaches the heart of their audiences. One of the highlights is the chapter on "The Perfect Opening," which easily lays out the seven steps to a perfect opening, one of the most important parts of any presentation.

Hoff, Ron, *I Can See You Naked: A Fearless Guide to Making Great Presentations.* Kansas City, Mo.: Andrews and McMeel, 1988. Ron's fast-paced book contains interesting and humorous anecdotes and helpful "nuggets" to help you be a better presenter.

Holcomb, Jane, Ph.D. *Making Training Worth Every Penny.* Del Mar, Calif.: Wharton Publishing, 1993. If your presentations involve training, this book will provide you with a wealth of information on how to increase the likelihood that what people have learned in your training session will be applied effectively on the job. The section on "Methods for Evaluation" shows how to take a simple tool, the On-Target Evaluation Chart, and determine which of nine evaluation and follow-up methods will be most effective in your specific circumstances.

Mager, Robert F. Belmont, Calif.: Lake Publishing Co. Any book by Bob Mager is a worthwhile learning experience as well as a pure delight to read. The following titles are especially appropriate for people who want to improve their effectiveness as presenters.

——————. *Preparing Instructional Objectives* is a revised edition of the classic work that established behavioral rather than content-oriented learning objectives.

——————. *Measuring Instructional Results or Got a Match?* helps you develop the special tools you need to measure educational results. It shows you how to create a match between your teaching objectives and your measurement tools.

——————. *Developing Attitude Toward Learning or SMATs 'n' SMUTs* focuses on getting your audience excited about your subject, anxious to use what they've learned, and eager to know more.

Pearce, Terry. *Leading Out Loud: The Authentic Speaker, the Credible Leader.* San Francisco: Jossey-Bass, 1995. The basic premise of this book is that "speaking is a vital part of leadership." The chapter on "Connecting with Your Audience" focuses on two approaches—questions and stories—as powerful vehicles to establish a connection that will increase the probability that your audience will respond positively to your message.

Pike, Robert W. *Creative Training Techniques Handbook, 2nd Edition.* Minneapolis, Minn.: Lakewood Books, 1994. Bob Pike is the guru of creative training. This revised edition of a training classic is the most complete set of tools we know of related to the human technology of training. His section on group involvement by itself is worth much more than the purchase price of the book.

————. *High Impact Presentations* is a wonderful guide to making creative and powerful presentations. Outlined in a workbook-style format, this book includes the basic concepts of MindMapping as an effective technique for organizing your material.

Rozakis, Laurie and Robert Ko Heady. *The Complete Idiot's Guide to Speaking in Public with Confidence.* New York: Macmillan, 1995. From the title alone, you can tell this book combines seriousness and fun. It covers all aspects of making presentations from writing to delivering a speech. In addition to the explanation and teaching, this book provides helpful tips that are humorously set apart from the text under headings "Bet You Didn't Know," "Words to the Wise," "Tell Me About It," and "Word Power."

Scannell, Edward E., and John W. Newstrom. *Even More Games Trainers Play.* New York: McGraw-Hill, 1994. This is the fourth in the popular *Games Trainers Play* series. This book, like its predecessors, is chock full of interactive exercises to get audiences loosened up and involved in what you are doing. The games listed under "Creative Problem Solving" are especially useful when you want your audience to actively participate in addressing critical issues related to your subject.

Schloff, Laurie, and Marcia Yudkin. *Smart Speaking.* New York: Plume Publishers, 1991. This is a fast-reading and informative book that is designed so you can dive in anywhere and find quick assistance for your urgent communication problems. Topics cover the areas from the sound of your voice, developing presentations on the run to meetings, and tough speaking situations. The authors keep their suggestions brief and to the point; a lot of valuable information is broken down into brief, easy-to-read points.

Slutsky, Jeff, and Michael Aun, *The Toastmasters International® Guide to Successful Speaking.* Chicago: Dearborn Financial Publishing, Inc., 1997. Jeff Slutsky, and Michael Aun are two of the most effective professional speakers on the platform today. They have put together a delightful book on speaking basics that is chock full of tips and resources. The chapters on "Using Humor to Make Your Point" and "Engaging Effective Audience Participation" are especially useful for those who want to add that "something special" that makes a good speech great.

Snyder, Marilyn A. *High-Performance Speaking.* Burr Ridge, Ill.: Irwin Professional Publishing, 1995. A strong proponent of interactive speaking and training, Marilyn Snyder has written this thought-provoking book in an interactive style. The chapter "Humor: Bring Them Back Alive!" provides an excellent format for creating and delivering appropriate humor in your presentation.

Valenti, Jack, *Speak Up with Confidence.* New York: Morrow, 1982. Valenti, a well-known figure in the entertainment industry, presents in this classic text many ideas for building confidence when speaking.

von Oech, Roger. *A Kick in the Seat of the Pants.* New York: Harper and Row, 1986. von Oech, the noted creativity guru, suggests ways for tapping the power of the right side of the brain, useful in many ways for incorporating creative approaches to presenting information formally and informally.

Walters, Dottie, and Lillet Walters. *Speak and Grow Rich.* Englewood Cliffs, N.J.: Prentice-Hall, 1989. If you have been toying with the idea of becoming a professional speaker, this

book, written by two pros who know that business, is the one
you need to get. It covers everything from how to get started
to effective promotion to development and sale of speaker
products.

Walters, Lilly. *What to Say When . . . You're Dying on the Platform.*
New York: McGraw-Hill, 1995. Anyone who has had to speak
before groups has had their share of moments when nothing
seems to go right. In this book, Lilly Walters has distilled the
wisdom and experience of several professional speakers in
producing this treasure trove of ideas for dealing with almost
every conceivable situation. It's a fun book to read in addition
to providing some powerful ways to anticipate and address
those circumstances you are likely to face.

OTHER RESOURCES

Software

There are many software packages that can help presenters prepare
anything from simple, quick presentation support materials to
multimedia "shows" involving complex content. Many presenters
have a "favorite"; some maintain a list of programs "they would
never use"; others haven't a clue about how to use software to help
with presentations. While the following list is by no means totally
inclusive, it does contain the more popular and prominent presentation packages used by the vast majority of presenters. Many of
these programs are available in demonstration format for down-
loading from the World Wide Web.

Adobe® Persuasion™ helps presenters create, manage, and deliver
presentations incorporating multimedia capabilities (sounds,
video clips, animation, instant branching to related slides),
easily working on both PC and Macintosh platforms. *Adobe
Systems, Inc.,* P.O. Box 6458, Salinas, CA 93912.
http://www.adobe.com

Astound™ is a good choice for users who want more sophisticated multimedia capabilities in their presentation software. Editing tools are intuitive and support drag-and-drop and OLE. *Astound, Inc.,* 3160 Bayshore Road, Palo Alto, CA 94303. http://www.astound.com

Corel® *Presentations for Windows*™ provides tools you need to present your ideas quickly and effectively, no matter what your level of expertise. It's easy to learn and use and integrates fully with other applications. Contains more than 60 slide backgrounds, special effects, and clip-art images to help you create sophisticated presentations in record time. *Corel Inc.,* 1600 Carling Ave. Ottawa, Ontario, Canada, K1Z 8R7. http://www.corel.com

Harvard Graphics™, by Software Publishing Corp., is designed for people who are using other products, such as spreadsheets and word processing, to create their visuals, and includes the innovative Adviser Design Checker to give feedback on a presentation's design. SPC has also developed ASAP Word Power™, which uses SPC's Intelligent Formatting™ to create compelling presentation reports and handouts in minutes. *Software Publishing Corporation,* 111 North Market Street, San Jose, CA 95113. http://www.spco.com

Lotus® *Freelance*™ is a fully integrated business graphics package that is part of *Lotus*® *SmartSuite*™. It offers a fast way to create plans, reports, and proposals that double as presentations. *Lotus Development Corporation,* 55 Cambridge Parkway, Cambridge, MA 02142. http://www.lotus.com

Microsoft® *PowerPoint*™ is one of the easiest presentation packages to use, with AutoContent Wizards and an internal clip-art library that contains lots of graphics for insertion into presentations. Bundled with *Microsoft*® *Office*™, it takes full advantage of word processing and spreadsheet compatibility. *Microsoft Corporation,* One Microsoft Way, Redmond, WA 98052. http://www.microsoft.com

Magazines/Newsletters

Creative Training Techniques™ Newsletter. Lakewood Publications, 50 South Ninth Street, Minneapolis, MN 55402. Edited by Bob Pike, this publication includes easy-to-learn, inexpensive, and effective tips, tactics, and techniques that enliven training and improve end results. It's designed for professionals at every experience level—from full-time professionals to occasional trainers to managers and executives who make frequent presentations.

Presentations Magazine, Lakewood Publications. This magazine brings you the expert intelligence you need to make better presentations and more cost-effective decisions about the products you select. It provides monthly how-to tips, techniques, new technologies, case studies, and more.

Sharing Ideas Newsmagazine, P.O. Box 1120, Glendora, CA 91740. Edited by Dottie Walters, this publication provides a wealth of news, information, techniques, and services designed to help speakers become more knowledgeable and effective.

Audio/Video

Be Prepared to Speak. Toastmasters International Communication Series. San Francisco: Kantola Productions. This is an excellent, reasonably priced, step-by-step Video Guide to Public Speaking that is divided into three areas: speechwriting, speech presentation, and overcoming stage fright. The information is presented in an interesting format, following a story that moves from a person who reluctantly accepts a speaking engagement to the final successful presentation.

Creative Training Techniques™ Newsletter in Action video series. Lakewood Publications. This three-volume series shows Bob Pike in action as he demonstrates his top training tips, tactics, and how-tos.

Decker, Bert. *You've Got to Be Believed to Be Heard,* audiotape program. Audio Renaissance, 1992. Based on the popular book, this is an innovative program filled with practical exercises designed to transform the way one speaks—and achieves.

Hessert, Kathleen, *Loud and Clear: Replace the Voice You Have with the Voice You Need; What I Meant Was . . . Making Media Interviews Work for You;* and *Strong Language: Using Language for More Power,* audiotape programs, Charlotte, N.C.: Communication Concepts (704) 365-5027, 1987. This three-part audio cassette program covers a wide range of communication topics and exercises. Each part comes with a workbook that can be used along with the tapes. For the presenter, the *Loud and Clear* part identifies common voice weaknesses and presents exercises that will help fine tune these areas. The articulation exercises are a great way to fine tune your diction. For those who are frequently interviewed by the media, *What I Meant Was . . .* offers specific information on handling the media, surviving ambush interviews, and dealing with crisis communication situations. *Strong Language* focuses on commonly used language that diminishes the power of a message. Throughout the program, Kathleen provides practical exercises to add impact to any type of communication.

Associations

American Society for Training and Development. 1640 King Street, Box 1443, Alexandria, VA 22313-2043, (800) 424-9106. This is the largest association in the world serving professionals in the training and development field. In addition to its national and regional meetings and many publications, it has a large network of local chapters. Check its web site for further information. http://www.astd.org.

National Speakers Association, 1500 So. Priest Drive, Tempe, AZ 85281, (602) 968-2552. This 4,000-plus member association provides a wealth of services and publications for professional speakers, including an annual convention, educational workshops, learning laboratories, on-line research services, monthly print and audiotape magazines, and approximately 40 local chapters. Check its web site for further information. http://www.nsaspeaker.org.

Toastmasters International, P.O. Box 9052, Mission Viejo, CA 92688, (714) 858-8255. The largest organization designed to help people become more effective speakers, Toastmasters has hundreds of chapters represented in every state in the United States and many countries throughout the world. Check its web site for further information. http://www.toastmasters.org.

About the Authors

George L. Morrisey, CSP, CPAE

George Morrisey is recognized throughout the world as one of the foremost experts in the field of strategic and tactical planning. He has more than twenty years' experience as a practicing manager and key specialist with First Western Bank, Rockwell International, McDonnell Douglas, the U.S. Postal Service, and the YMCA, in addition to more than twenty-five years as a full-time consultant, professional speaker, and seminar leader. He is the chairman of The Morrisey Group, a management consulting firm based in Merritt Island, Florida. He received his B.S. and M.Ed. degrees from Springfield (Mass.) College. He has personally assisted more than 200 business, industrial, service, governmental, and not-for-profit organizations throughout the world, including Atwood Mobile Products, BHP Minerals, Burger King, Iowa State Governor's Office, John Deere Credit, Kuwait Petroleum Corporation, NASA, Recreation Vehicle Industry Association, and the U.S. Department of Agriculture.

He is the author or co-author of eighteen books prior to this one, including *Morrisey on Planning*, a three-book series on strategic thinking, long-range planning, and tactical planning, published by Jossey-Bass in 1996. His other Addison-Wesley books are *Management by Objectives and Results for Business and Industry*, *Management by Objectives and Results in the Public Sector*, *Performance Appraisals for Business and Industry*, *Performance Appraisals in the Public Sector*, and the earlier editions of *Effective Business and Technical Presentations*. Additional published works include *Creating Your Future: Personal Strategic Planning for Professionals, Getting Your Act Together: Goal Setting for Fun, Health and Profit, The Executive Guide to Strategic Planning,* and *The Executive Guide to Operational Planning.* He is the author and producer of several audio- and videocassette learning programs, all directed toward helping individuals and organizations become more effective and self-fulfilled.

A professional's professional, George Morrisey received the Certified Speaking Professional (CSP) designation in 1983 and was recognized in 1984 with CPAE (Council of Peers Award for Excellence), the highest recognition granted to a professional speaker by the National Speakers Association. In addition, in 1994, George was the 16th annual recipient of the Cavett Award, named in honor of that association's founder, Cavett Robert. He is formerly a member of the Boards of Directors of the Association for Management Excellence (originally the International MBO Institute) and the National Speakers Association.

For further information on George Morrisey's services, please contact:

The Morrisey Group
P.O. Box 541296
Merritt Island, FL 32954-1296
(800) 535-8202, (407) 452-7414, Fax (407) 452-2129
World Wide Web: http://www.morrisey.com
Email: gmorrisey@aol.com

Thomas L. Sechrest, M.S.

Tom Sechrest has been involved in adult learning and development for over twenty years, as an educational and industrial television producer, in various management and organization-development capacities for the federal government, and as an independent consultant. At mid-life and in mid-career, Tom went "back to school" at The University of Texas at Austin, where he is completing the requirements for his doctoral degree in Human Resource Development in one of the nation's most highly recognized professional programs. He served as a Research and Teaching Assistant in Human Resource Development, and managed international conferences and seminars for the Continuing Education Program at The University of Texas, where he refined a global systems perspective and gained an international clientele for his seminars in leadership and technology. He currently is the Senior Learning and Development Specialist for Leadership and Management Development Programs at Advanced Micro Devices, Inc., a global supplier of integrated circuits for the personal and networked computer and communications markets, located in Austin.

Tom is the author and editor of academic works in educational technology, program planning, systems thinking, and leadership development. He is a member of the Academy of Human Resource Development and the National University Continuing Education Association and is an officer on the Board of Directors of the Austin Chapter of the American Society for Training and Development. He serves as Administrative Director of the Institute for Organization and Human Resource Development and advisor to The University of Texas Chapter of Beta Theta Pi General Fraternity.

For further information, please contact:

Thomas L. Sechrest and Associates
504 West 24th Street, Suite 83
Austin, TX 78705-5231
(512) 442-4150, Fax: (512) 442-0341
Email: tom.sechrest@amd.com

Wendy B. Warman, M.S.

Wendy Warman is owner and President of SmarTalkers, a training and consulting firm located in Clearwater, Florida. A certified speech pathologist, seminar leader, professional speaker, and author, she is best known for her expertise as a speech and voice coach and for the seminars and workshops on communication skills she conducts for such organizations as Alliance Business Centers Network; Honeywell; Cargill; Smith and Nephew United; Barnett Bank; A.G. Edwards; Lokey Motor Company; Salomon Brothers; Hoffman-LaRoche; and Florida Power Corporation.

Wendy has a Master of Science degree in Speech Pathology and brings more than twenty-one years of research and experience in the field of communications to her clients. She has served as President of the Central Florida Speakers Association and is an active member of the National Speakers Association, American Society for Training and Development, and the American Speech and Hearing Association.

For further information on Wendy Warman's services, please contact:

SmarTalkers
P.O. Box 4611
Clearwater, FL 34618-4611
(813) 441-9858, Fax (813) 461-2727
Email: Smartalker@aol.com

Audio Visual Innovations

The many examples of presentation visuals in *Loud and Clear* were created by Audio Visual Innovations, Inc., of Tampa, Florida. Since 1979 AVI has provided audiovisual and presentation technology, training, and expertise to help its clients stand out from the crowd.

Audio Visual Innovations is one of the largest resellers of LCD and DLP projection systems in the United States. The services that AVI offers include custom design and installation of audiovisual equipment for board rooms, training rooms, and conference rooms; rental and meeting support services; repairs; and extended warranties. AVI's graphic experts work with clients to develop visuals and other support materials that take full advantage of their technology and spice up any presentation.

For value, selection, service, and support, call Audio Visual Innovations. AVI has offices in Tampa, Orlando, Jacksonville, Miami, and Tallahassee, Florida; Mobile and Huntsville, Alabama; and Charleston, South Carolina. For further information on AVI's products and services, please contact its main office:

Audio Visual Innovations, Inc.
6313 Benjamin Road, Suite 110
Tampa, FL 32216
(800) 282-6733, (813) 884-7168, Fax: (813) 882-9508
World Wide Web: http://www.aviinc.com
Email: avi@aviinc.com